Life's Little Rituals

D0958539

Life's Little ❀ Rituals ❀

Celebrations for Everyday Living

ALEXANDRIA

CITADEL PRESS
Kensington Publishing Corp.
www.kensingtonbooks.com

CITADEL PRESS BOOKS are published by

Kensington Publishing Corp.
850 Third Avenue
New York, NY 10022

All Kensington titles, imprints, and distributed lines are available at special quantity discounts for bulk purchases for sales promotions, premiums, fund-raising, educational, or institutional use. Special book excerpts or customized printings can also be created to fit specific needs. For details, write or phone the office of the Kensington special sales manager: Kensington Publishing Corp., 850 Third Avenue, New York, NY 10022, attn: Special Sales Department; phone 1-800-221-2647.

CITADEL PRESS and the Citadel logo are Reg. U.S. Pat. & TM Off.

First printing: August 2004

10 9 8 7 6 5 4 3 2 1

Printed in the United States of America

Library of Congress Control Number: 2004106001

ISBN 0-8065-2605-X

To my Mother, Barbara White

Thank you for teaching me that
every day can be a celebration.
From you I learned to live life to the fullest.

I love you.

Contents

Preface

What is a ritual? According to *Webster's*:

rit·u·al *noun*　**1 :** the established form especially for a religious ceremony

This definition is pretty self-explanatory. It is what you experience at your place of worship every time you attend.

2 : a system of rites

This is what takes place during religious gatherings or special occasions. Those special occasions include religious holidays like Christmas, Passover, Summer Solstice, or Ramadan. Christenings, weddings, and funerals are also considered "a system of rites." The specific liturgy and traditional prayers that accompany these and other special religious occasions are also included in this definition.

3 : a ceremonial act or action

Placing your hand over your heart during the Pledge of Allegiance and flying the flag during national holidays are both examples of ceremonial acts. Blowing out the candles on a birthday cake is an action that is ceremonial in nature, too.

4 : a customarily repeated act or series of acts

This one is a little more difficult to define. It could be as simple as the order in which you get ready for bed (brush teeth, wash face, put on pj's, set alarm), or as complex as making dinner from scratch every evening.

Ritualizing daily life is living with conscious intent. Instead of walking through life like a zombie, this book actually encourages us to think about and put meaning into our daily lives. We often tend to zone out and not even *think* about what is occurring during our day. When we do this, time flies by and, before we know it, the days are passing like hours, the months like days, and eventually, the years begin to feel like months. It doesn't take a lot of effort or a major lifestyle change to bring meaning back into our lives. All it takes is awareness and making everything we do into a ritual. We already have a lot more rituals in our lives than we think, and this book will show you a few more.

Definition 1: *the established form especially for a religious ceremony* and definition 2: *a system of rites* are established by your own religious beliefs, so they will not be included in this book. I do not wish to favor any particular religion and researching all of them would fill an entire wall with books. As a matter of fact, there are whole libraries devoted to the liturgy, rites, and traditional ceremonies of every organized religion there is.

Definition 3: *a ceremonial act or action* and definition 4: *a customarily repeated act or series of acts* describe the rituals you will find in this book. Creating ceremonies and celebrations for the everyday events in our lives is what *Life's Little*

Rituals is all about. Have you ever heard of a ritual for a first date? How about one for being stuck in traffic? Dating? Losing your job? Starting a workout routine? The first snow-fall of Winter? Maybe creating rituals for these things sounds silly to you. Well, some of the rituals in this book are *intentionally* silly. You will also find serious rituals that celebrate the milestones in life we tend to forget about in the rush of everyday life.

Most of the rituals in this book are simple actions with only a few words that take very little time, but the feelings invoked will last much longer.

These rituals are also designed to provoke thought and bring more meaning into your everyday life. Follow them to the letter, use them as templates, or make up your own. Let's see just how much fun you can have every day!

The meaning of life is a life filled with meaning!

Acknowledgments

Writing a book is like a raising a child; it definitely takes a village. In my village there are many I would like to thank. Let's start with my own household. To my husband, Stephen Fishman, thank you, sweetheart, for pushing me beyond my comfort zone. You always knew what I needed most, even when I didn't. To my mom, Barbara White, thank you for listening to rough first drafts and offering suggestions on how they could be better. I believe in you just as much as you believe in me. To my sister, Lisa Payne, thanks for letting me rant when I needed it and for supporting me in my efforts, both book-related and not.

Moving on down the road, I want to thank my closest neighbors, the ones who provided emotional support and so much more. To Charlie S., thank you for your friendship, encouragement, and words of wisdom. One of these days, you're going to have to send me a bill. To Jeanette Waldie and Carla, thank you for giving me your unique views of parenthood. Since I have no children of my own, it would have been difficult to complete that section without your help. To Mary Wolf, friend and teacher, your confidence in me was a real boost when my enthusiasm flagged.

Then there are those to thank in the big building at the end of the street, Citadel Press. To my publisher, Bruce Bender, thank you for your undying patience and your belief in this project. To my editor, Margaret Wolf, thank you for your understanding and your diplomatic ways. It still amazes me how you can rearrange a few words and make what I have written sound so much better. And to your tireless assistant, Amanda Rouse, my thanks also. To the others at Citadel Press who worked on this book, my thanks for putting your best effort forward on my behalf.

I cannot forget the tireless communications system of this village, my agent Sara Camilli. Your understanding, patience, and sense of humor provided so much support I cannot even begin to measure it. Thank you for your continuing belief in me and in my words.

A special thanks must go to my spiritual brothers and sisters at CMA for encouraging me to grow beyond what I thought I was capable of. Last of all, I would like to thank the village as a whole, all my friends and family that are too numerous to list here. Thank you all for your ongoing love, honor, and support. I love you all!

Life's Little Rituals

1

Everyday Stuff

IT'S THE EVERYDAY activities in our lives that need to be ritu-
alized the most. This chapter includes rituals for those
everyday actions—from brushing our teeth in the morning,
rushing through chores, finishing a good book, meals, and
bedtime. Most of the rituals in this section are quickies
because we all already have established routines in our lives.
I start this book with the shorter rituals so you can see how
simple a ritual can be. In later chapters some of the rituals
will get slightly more complex, but by then you will have
gotten the gist of rituals in general. The purpose of this chapter is to increase your awareness of everyday routines and
enable you to live life more mindfully.

Coming Home

Coming home should be joyful. Home is a place of relaxation,
fun, and comfort. Yes, we have household chores, but they
are labors of love, for they make our home more comfortable and inviting. And when there is love in a home, we tend
not to notice the dust or the clutter. For a while anyway. A

quiet ritual of homecoming shuts out work, errands, and the stresses of the outside world and prepares you to truly "be at home." This is an attitude that not only you will appreciate, but your loved ones will as well. Ready for that attitude adjustment? Here goes.

Take a few moments before you walk through the door, whether that door is in the front, the back, or the garage, and stand very still. Take a deep breath, then let it out with a sigh. An audible sigh helps release tension in the body. Sigh as many times as it takes to get your shoulders to come down out of your ears, and relax. Say any of the following clichés (or make up your own), either to yourself or aloud as you walk through the door.

> *Home Sweet Home*
> *Home Is Where the Heart Is*
> *Be it ever so humble,*
> *There's No Place Like Home*
> *Home is where you hang your hat.*
> *A man's home is his castle.*

It may sound silly, I know. And it may *feel* silly the first few times you do it. On the other hand, is silly such a bad thing? Isn't fun one of the things home is supposed to be about? So be a little silly, and welcome home!

Morning and Bedtime Routine

Our morning and bedtime routines are extremely personal, and the way we *start* the day determines our attitude for the *rest* of the day. "Getting up on the wrong side of the bed" is an expression that speaks directly to being in a bad mood all day because you've had a break in your routine. Whatever your personal routine is, it is important to follow it so you don't end up grouchy all day. However . . . (you knew there was going to be a however) an *occasional* break in routine can make you feel more alive. The down side to routines is that they tend to put us on automatic, creating that mindlessness I mentioned in the introduction. That mindlessness brings our energy levels down and causes one day to blur into the next. So here is a ritual designed to break you out of your normal routine without disrupting your life too terribly much.

Pick one day of the week that you will change your routine. What day that is makes less difference than remembering to do the following on that day *every* week. On that day (let's say Wednesday morning) instead of starting the coffee *before* you brush your teeth, do it after. If you find yourself going to the kitchen anyway, then you realize it's your day to be different; write yourself a sticky note and take it back to the bathroom with you. Place it on the mirror to remind you to start the coffee *after* your shower. It's going to feel weird, but don't let it stress you out. Of course, there are some things you shouldn't change; for example, taking your shower *after* you have gotten dressed could ruin your whole day.

A change in routine can completely change your outlook on the world and even stimulate your creativity. That's why we feel so refreshed after a vacation. It's not just the relaxation that comes from being away from work, it's also the break in routine that refreshes you. See the ritual "Vacation" in Chapter 6, "Hi-Ho, Hi-Ho, It's Off to Work We Go" (page 128).

When you find yourself getting used to this change in routine, it will be time to change it *again*. You can do this by either changing the day of the week or the order of something else—like washing your hair in the shower *before* you lather your body instead of after.

By changing your routine, you just may find that you work better on those days, because you are actually thinking about what you are doing instead of just going through the motions.

Laundry Day and Chores

Have you ever wondered how the term "Blue Monday" originated? Most people think it comes from the depressed state of going back to work after two days off. In actuality the phrase Blue Monday came from a time when Mondays were laundry day. Bluing was used in the water to help counteract the yellowing of laundered fabrics, so Blue Monday was an expression that meant laundry day. Now for me (someone who *hates* doing laundry) the blue part of Blue Monday has multiple meanings and one of them is being "down" about doing the laundry. Chores in general bring most people down, because most chores are repetitive and boring. So try the following rituals to liven things up a little.

These quickies are definitely on the silly side, but I am of the opinion that the more boring the task, the more silly should be the ways you deal with it.

Turn on the radio and teach yourself a new dance step while sweeping the floor.

Mop the floor in a spiral by starting in the middle and working your way out. You could do the opposite, but it would tend to leave footprints all over your freshly mopped floor and that's counterproductive.

When you vacuum, finish up by vacuuming a design in the carpet. Vary the design every time. Ask your kids for suggestions for designs.

Play tic-tac-toe or draw pictures in the dust before you sweep it away.

Read a romance novel (even if you don't like them) while listening to the washing machine or dryer. It adds a great soundtrack.

When you fold clean clothes add little notes like "love you," or "smile." Cut out a funny cartoon or draw a cute picture and add those to the stacks. Your loved ones will be delighted. Don't forget to do it for yourself, also. Finding a note that says, "You look terrific!" on a day when you are feeling down will liven you right up.

Use spray cleaners like you would use spray paint and paint pictures on your countertops before wiping away spills. See how creative you can get by incorporating those spills into your "artwork."

If you are lucky enough to be able to share your chores, turn them into a competition. Can Janie finish vacuuming before Jackie completes the dusting? Develop a point system and take points off for sloppy or incomplete work. Add points for creativity. Have prizes. The winner gets ice cream for an afternoon snack.

Above all, try to have fun with your chores. It makes them go a lot faster and is much more entertaining. Especially if someone is watching!

Meals

In our hectic society, few of us take the time to actually sit down and have a meal. Oh, we eat, but mostly just to sustain ourselves. Holidays seem to be the only break in this routine. What we forget is that meals can be a great time for conversation, especially in large families. It's easy to forget to "check in" with each other if everyone is on different eating schedules. A meal should be a ritual. And that ritual is one that revolves around family and is all about connectedness. I know it's difficult to find the time. If it seems impossible to have a sit down meal every night, try to do it at least once a week. When the whole family does sit down to a meal, use this ritual to enhance the experience.

Once everyone is seated at the table and has food in front of them, some people say grace or give thanks for the food. This ritual is along those same lines, but it has no religious flavor. If you say grace, this ritual can be included in the prayer. It could also be said either before or after saying grace.
    Before beginning your meal, say the following:

> *We gather to share food and conversation.*
> *Our lives are enhanced by each person sitting*
>   *at this table.*
> *We are grateful to be able to share food with those*
>   *we love.*
> *May our lives be as abundant as the food on our*
>   *table.*

    Take turns each time and encourage family members to personalize the saying. For example, each family member can speak aloud about something that has happened during that day or that week for which they are grateful—getting an A on a test, completing a project at work, or being with loved ones. These subjects can also be great conversation starters for later in the meal or for after dinner.

Feel free to change the wording to something that makes you comfortable. *Bon appétit!*

There's Nothing Like a Good Book

Grab a glass of iced tea, turn off the phone, put your feet up, and relax. It's time to get completely absorbed in a good book. Reading a novel is like watching a movie, except instead of going to a theater or watching it on television, we see it playing in our minds. We do the casting, run the cameras, call it quits for the day, or decide to redo a scene that just doesn't look right. Or, if we like a scene, it's easy to hit the rewind button and watch it again and again just by turning back a few pages and rereading those pages as many times as we like. And it just plain feels good to hold a book and turn the pages. Taking a favorite book to the beach or on a picnic is a great joy. Even surrounded by strangers on a bus or train, we can completely escape into the events of someone else's life, and fiction isn't the only escape either. Biographies, histories, even how-to books can provide a way to forget about an awful day or enhance different aspects of our lives. Reading a book is, in itself, a ritual. It is a ritual of relaxation. To enhance *that* ritual, try these short rituals.

When starting a new book, make sure you will be uninterrupted for at least an hour, so you can get a good start on the story.

When picking up a book you have already started, reread the page previous to where you left off. It will get you back into the story with minimal effort.

Finishing a book is a little bit of a letdown; especially if it was a very good one. It's like saying good-bye to a new group of friends. On that occasion, pour yourself a beverage (adult or otherwise), toast the characters, and wish them bon voyage.

Now, on to the next great adventure!

Voting

Voting is a ritual in and of itself. In a democratic society, voting ensures freedom. We engage in political discourse then vote for or against people, their ideologies, and the projects they have put before us. I feel most patriotic on the days I vote and I am thankful that I live in a society I have a hand in creating. This small ritual of thankfulness celebrates the idea of "one person, one vote" and should be done on the day you cast your vote.

On your way to vote, keep this fact in mind: For seventy-two years women fought for the right to vote, and in August 1920 that right was finally won, by *one vote*! The 19th Amendment was ratified and became the law of the land because of *one vote*! Your vote does count, and that fact proves it. Sometimes it takes years and several generations to overcome an injustice or to get a law changed. Perseverance counts—and so does your voice.

After you have cast your vote drink a toast to the power of one vote and revel in democracy.

Leaving Home

Most of us leave home, at least temporarily, over the course of our daily lives. This ritual is complementary to the coming-home ritual.

It's a good idea to have an eye-catching sign just inside the door that you will notice before you leave. It can read: "Think" or "Did you. . . ?" When you have your keys in your hand, stop at this sign for a moment. Run through a mental checklist and make sure all devices such as irons and stoves are turned off. Did you remember to check and adjust the thermostat? Are there clothes that need to be taken to the cleaners? Do you need anything special for work or school?

After you've run through your checklist, close your eyes and consciously "feel" your home around you. Take a few moments to imagine the walls as protective and comforting arms around you and know that they will be there waiting for you when you return.

As you set the alarm, lock the door behind you, or put the garage door down, visualize the exterior of your home as a giant enclosed shell keeping out all intruders. Safe journeys!

2

ℋome on the ℛange

SAFETY, COMFORT, LOVE, PEACE—all come to mind when thinking about home. This chapter is about the events that happen at home and how we can celebrate our special space. The following rituals will help make your house into more than just a place to eat, sleep, and store your stuff. Celebrations of new furniture, pets, parties, and roommates make your house into a home.

New Home

Moving into a new space, whether it is an apartment, town home, house, or cabin in the country, is exciting. But it is not truly your own until you make it that way. Ritual is especially important in a new living space. It is needed to help you feel comfortable from day one. I've included several rituals for you in your new home. Choose one, two, or all of them to welcome you home.

* * *

We all have special objects in our lives—a favorite painting, chair, or dish. . . . It could be something handed down for generations or something you found at a crafts fair last year. Think about that object in your life that speaks directly to your heart, and don't pack it away. Instead, place it in your new space before anything else has been moved in. One good place to display it is on your mantle, because fireplaces and hearths have been considered since ancient times to be the heart of the house. By placing an object that is special to you in the heart of your house, you are symbolically melding your heart with that of your new home. In our modern times, kitchens often take the place of the fireplaces of old; they are often the emotional centers of our lives for much the same reasons—warmth, community, and food. If you don't have a fireplace or your kitchen doesn't feel right, find a place of honor that is just as significant. While you are laboring to put everything away, you can focus on this object and you will know in your heart that you are at home.

Most of us actually have our new space for at least a day or two before we move in. While your new space is still empty of furnishings, have a meal in the bare space. Food represents comfort, wealth, and prosperity. As you eat, go through each room and imagine what will go where and visualize the activities that will take place in each room. Leave a small piece of bread and pour a sip of your drink on the doorstep of your home as you are leaving and say:

> *Joy and abundance reside at my doorstep and*
>   *beyond.*
> *May it touch all who enter this dwelling.*

Housewarming parties are another great ritual. Friends and family members add their own special touch to our lives by providing the new space with plants or other decorative objects, laughter, and fun. To add a unique touch to your housewarming party, have paper and pens available to everyone there. Have each guest write down something that they wish for you in your new home. Then ask them to hide their wishes throughout the house during the course of the party. Make sure to tell them not to make the papers too hard to find, but to be creative with the hiding places. Rolled up in a glass in the pantry, tucked between towels in the linen closet, or stuck in drawers are all suggestions you can make to your guests for hiding places.

Over the next few days and weeks, you will be finding good wishes throughout your home. What a great way not only to feel comfortable in your new space, but also to know how much you are loved and wished happiness.

Enjoy your new home. May it be a haven of peace and joy for all who reside there.

New Furniture

It's so wonderful to have new furniture! Picking out something we love is easy. Integrating it into our home is the challenging part. Sometimes new furniture speaks loudly and lets you know where it belongs in a room. Most of the time, though, it's not that easy. This ritual will help you find a place for that new sofa or armoire and, at the same time, make it seem like a part of the family from the moment you bring it through the door.

* * *

When you buy antique furniture or something from a yard sale, it's a given that it has been owned before. This can make some people very uncomfortable. If you are one of those people, try the following. Immediately before moving the piece inside the house, stand outside the door for a moment. Imagine a waterfall flowing from the top of the house and cascading over the doorway. Visualize the waterfall washing away any negative associations as you move the piece under the waterfall and into the house.

Place the furniture in the spot you want it, then take a few minutes to speak about the purpose of the piece. For example, if it's a bed for the master bedroom you might say that the purpose of the piece is for sleep, relaxation, and love. If it's a new toy box for one of the kids, tell the child that this box is to keep all that child's toys safe and protect them from damage. You could even elaborate and tell the child that the box will only keep toys safe if they are put into it when they are not being used. This will encourage your child to put away the toys in order to keep them safe. If it's a new entertainment center, state the purpose as a source of entertainment and knowledge. A new computer is for learning and fun. You get the idea.

Now your new piece of furniture has its purpose. This will help you feel more comfortable with the piece from the beginning. If you can't seem to find the right spot for the new piece, you may have to rearrange your old furniture in order to accommodate it. When you do this, restate the purpose of the pieces you are moving. Congratulations on your new furniture. May it bring you years of enjoyment.

Last, but not least, don't forget to turn off the waterfall.

Party Time

Woo hoo! It's party time. Whether you like to give elaborate dinner parties or just hang out with friends, party time is definitely meant for fun. Friends and family bring so much joy into our lives that there needs to be more to the celebration than just the celebration itself. No matter what the occasion try this ritual before each party.

If the thought of ritual makes your friends and family members uncomfortable you can do this ritual on your own before they arrive. If they are open minded, you might want to wait for them to arrive so they can participate. Buy a big bag of tea lights—super size if you give a lot of parties.
   For each person invited light a single candle and say:

> *This candle I light,*
> *Makes this friendship burn bright.*
> *It brightens my home as does the presence of*
>   [name of guest].

   If you have the same people over on a regular basis, you might want to have them each bring a large pillar-type candle to leave in your home. This candle will be a representation of the joy they bring into your life every time they enter your home, and each friend should light his personal candle each time he crosses your doorstep. This is a great way not only to kick off your party, but also to decorate the room.
   Party on!

New Car

There's nothing like that new-car smell. Wheels. Mobility. Freedom. This ritual celebrates all those things and more as well as helping you to feel protected while traveling.

The first thing you want to do is make the car your own. A favorite bumper sticker personalizes a car. So do steering wheel covers, personalized floor mats, or some small meaningful object dangling from the rearview mirror. Presetting your favorite radio stations and slipping that first CD into the player also make statements that this car belongs to you.

But a car is more than just an expression of personal taste, it's also a vehicle that gets us safely from point A to point B. Do this ritual in order to feel safe in your new car.

Sit in the driver's seat and pull the seat belt across your chest. As you do imagine that the seat belt is your mother's hand reaching across you. You will remember her hand holding you in as a child when she had to stop suddenly. Imagine the entire car as a comforting maternal presence, enclosing you in protective arms. When you first buy your car, sit quietly in a parking lot or in your garage and hold this vision in your head for several minutes. It is similar to the ritual "Leaving Home" in chapter 1, "Everyday Stuff" (page 9). Think of the protective arms of your car being an extension of the protective arms of your house; feel that presence every time you get into the car and fasten your seat belt.

Drive cheerfully!

New Roommate

A new roommate can sometimes unsettle you. You were used to your old roommate and her habits. Alarm clocks going off at certain times, morning routines, even music choices all vary from person to person. You're probably learning more than you want to know about that other person's habits. So when it's time for a new roommate, try this ritual to start things out on the right foot.

First of all, talk to your new roommate about both of your normal routines and habits, so you'll both know what to expect. Discuss expectations such as cleaning up after yourself, divisions in labor and chores, as well as money responsibilities—whatever else you can think of to smooth the way. After this "oh, so serious" talk, it's time to have some fun.

The beginning of this relationship is like the beginning of a voyage and there will be rough seas as well as clear sailing. It's time to have a bon voyage party to kick things off right. This can be as simple as tissue paper leis for two and a toast to each other or as complex as a full-blown party with luau decorations, confetti streamers, and drinks served from a steamer trunk. Whatever you decide, make sure that your new roomie feels welcome by clearing out refrigerator and bathroom shelves.

Good luck, and may the wind be always at your back and may you be greeted each day with fair skies.

New Pet

Bringing a new pet into our lives gives us a chance to experience unconditional love. The care and feeding of another living creature is a responsibility that must not be taken lightly. We become members of a dog's pack or a cat's pride when we open our homes to them. So we are not only bringing home a new pet, we are bringing home a new family member—and that family member needs to feel like a part of its new environment. This ritual welcomes an animal companion into the home.

Food, comfort, and attention—these three things are essential to the health of any animal you may bring home. When you first bring your animal home, have these three things waiting. Take the animal, preferably in a carrier, to the room where it will be sequestered for its first few days in your home. Walk slowly—it's important that the animal has sufficient time to take in its new surroundings; it will already be overwhelmed by new sights, sounds, and smells. Once you reach the animal's sanctuary, remove it from the carrier and hold it in your arms for a few moments. As you gently stroke the animal, say:

> *You are welcome in this home and will always*
> *be loved.*

Have a bed for your new pet in addition to a toy or two. Put an old pillowcase that you have slept on in your pet's bed; this will help it get used to your scent. While still holding the animal, show it the bed and say:

*This space is yours and yours alone. May it
provide comfort.*

Set the animal down in front of a bowlful of food and say:

In this home, you will never hunger.

Over the next few hours, have each member of the household enter the room and introduce himself or herself to the pet. The person who brought the new pet home should accompany each newcomer. Let the animal smell the hand of each newcomer before that person attempts to stroke it and repeat:

*You are welcome in this home and will always
be loved.*

The relationships between the new pet and the members of the household now have a good start. Spend quality time with your new pet to reinforce the intent you have set with your words. Training can begin once your new pet is comfortable in its surroundings. Be patient. Remember you are establishing a relationship that will last for years to come.

Loss of a Pet

It's terrible when a pet runs away or dies. The grief you feel is real to you even if it is not understood by others. When I lost a beloved cat to cancer, I heard comments like, "It's only a cat," or "You can always get another one." People who do not share their lives with animals may not understand the level of pain that accompanies the loss of a pet. Society, in general, does not acknowledge the importance of the grieving process when what's lost is "only" a pet. There are usually no funerals or memorial services, so I offer this short ritual to help ease the grief of losing something that has been such a large part of your life and has loved you unconditionally.

We tend to bottle up grief. The biggest problem with doing this is that if we do it long enough the container will eventually explode. Especially when it comes to grieving over something that others may deem unimportant. So, for this ritual you will need to find an empty bottle. It can be of any variety—an old wine bottle, a mayonnaise jar, or a soft drink container. Just make sure it has a cork or lid. You don't even have to take the label off, because you will be covering it up with a photo. That photo will be of your beloved pet that is now gone. Find a place for the bottle where you can leave it for a while. Place one of your pet's favorite toys next to the bottle. Make a shrine to your pet as elaborate or as simple as you wish. When that is done, set a time and schedule for your grief. Sounds strange, I know, but try it anyway.

Establish a time each day to grieve (for instance, when you get home from work or in the morning when you would normally be putting down food). Take the lid off the bottle and remember your pet. Imagine your grief pouring into the bottle and being contained there. If there are other family members, especially kids, have a family time to do this as well. Have each member of the family tell a favorite story or just sit silently. Let each family member know that it's okay to do this ritual anytime he or she is feeling sad. When you have finished your remembrances, place the lid back on the jar or bottle. There is no set time frame for this ritual, but, after a while, you will find that you forget to do the ritual or that the sorrow upon opening the bottle is not as great. You and your family members must determine how long the grieving process will last. It can be as short as a few days or as long as a year. In some cultures, grieving is considered officially over after a few days. In still others, people are expected to grieve for a year or more. Let your emotions determine the amount of *your* grieving time and you will eventually feel better. When you decide that the time for grieving is over, break or crush the bottle. By doing this, you are symbolically destroying your grief.

Always remember your pet with love and be thankful that it was part of your life, if only for a little while.

Moving

Moving is a time of great change. Gone are the days when many of us lived our whole lives in the same house or even the same town. We are a transient society on the move for a variety of reasons: jobs, schools, neighborhoods. We outgrow our houses as our family expands or we simply want a bigger place. Nicer neighborhoods beckon, or we want to live closer to work. All these reasons and more inspire us to change our addresses, but the hassle of packing and moving are time consuming and tiring. Try these entertaining rituals to ease the strain.

Before packing your first box, set in your mind that this is a *fun* process. That's right, I said *fun*! And the best way to make it fun is to remember the goal: to be settled and living in your new place. If possible, take photos of your new place and tape them up all over the house you are moving out of. This will give you a focus on the goal while you are packing. Whenever you feel bogged down, take a look at the picture nearest you. If you don't have pictures, a floor plan of your new space will also work. If neither of these are available, then use your imagination. Draw pictures with crayons or markers and post them instead. Anything you can use as a visual representation of your new space will help you focus on the goal. If you are moving to a new town, you can use pictures of that town or the recreational activities that it offers. Moving to the coast? Put up pictures of the beach. If you are moving to the mountains, put up pictures of skiing or hiking. Be creative.

As you pack, visualize where each item you are packing will be placed. This not only eases the burden of packing but makes it easier to label boxes for specific rooms and to unpack once you get moved.

Try to make packing fun by drawing pictures on the outside of the boxes. Purchase a big package of stickers from the store for each person packing, or use those wonderful crayons and markers, and have fun decorating the boxes. Make it personal. Try to save packing up your bedroom for last so you have a clean retreat while the rest of the house is in chaos.

On moving day make sure you have plenty of drinks for yourself and for the movers—hot chocolate or coffee if it's cold out and soft drinks or iced tea if it's warm. If your movers are friends, you will want to feed them as well. When the pizza (Chinese food, fried chicken) arrives, let everyone know that the day's "energy" has arrived. Eat with the intent that each bite provides you with both energy and enthusiasm.

Take a few minutes to relax after you eat. During this relaxation time, talk about the new place and your plans for it, then get back to work.

Like with the new car ritual earlier in this chapter, imagine the moving van as a maternal presence that will keep your stuff safe and secure while it is wrapped in giant metal arms.

Congrats, and have a safe and happy move.

3

Friends and Family

THIS CHAPTER is all about the people closest to us. Not just family, either—our friends and lovers as well. They are our family of choice and, as such, require just as much love and attention. Rituals, too! This chapter includes rituals designed specifically for help with the choices that come from the close relationships in our lives. Even though I will be using the traditional forms of family in this chapter, I am not attempting to leave anyone out. Those of you who are single parents, same-gender partners, and others who live "nontraditional" lifestyles, please accept the way the chapter is presented. It is not meant to exclude, only to describe the rituals as simply as possible. Feel free to modify them as needed. Blood may be thicker than water, but true friends are rare and require a bit more care.

New Friendship

It's such a blessing when we find a new friend. We are usually far into a new friendship before we even realize we have a friend. Suddenly, one day, we find ourselves in the middle of a conversation with someone and realize that we like the person and are talking in more than just a casual way. For whatever reason, someone new has touched our life and we will never be the same. An acquaintance has suddenly become a friend. Every new person who enters our lives teaches us something about ourselves. That calls for a celebration. Considering the person, you may or may not want to tell him or her that you consider the following suggestions to be ritualistic. I know I have friends who would freak out at the thought of being involved in a ritual. So I just say, "Hey, let's get together and. . . ."

There are many ways to celebrate a new friend:

Invite her to your favorite coffeehouse for dessert and swap your sweetest childhood memories.

Make dinner for your new friend. Sharing food is not only fun, it is also a great way to learn your friend's likes and dislikes—at least where food is concerned. Better yet, cook a meal together and imagine your friendship coming together as well as the different dishes in the meal do.

Suggest a day of marathon movie watching. Something that is a series is especially fun. *The Pink Panther*, *James Bond*, or *Star Wars* movies can be incredibly entertaining. If you pick a movie that you both have seen so many times that you know the dialogue by heart, it might be fun to turn down the volume and make up your *own*. I assure you it will have you both rolling on the floor with laughter.

Spend a day at the beach and talk about the kind of person whom you would find exciting. Point out examples from the people walking along the shore.

Barbecue and trade sauce recipes.

Read the same book, then get together to discuss it.

Each of you list your favorite things—from movies and ice cream flavors to songs. Swap lists.

Pick a movie that neither of you would typically see, then share your thoughts on it over a cup of coffee afterward. Praise it or pick it apart, but have reasons. Don't just say, "I hated it" or "I loved it." Try to discover the reasons why. If your friend feels the opposite, be open to his opinions as well. The best debates are between good friends.

Pick a place to have lunch that serves food neither of you have tried before, maybe Indian or Ethiopian. Try to identify the spices you might consider using. Discuss variations on the dish that you would prepare. You may find yourself returning often to this same place because you like it so well.

All of the above will help the two of you get to know each other better. As the friendship grows, you will find yourself happily remembering its early days.

Dating

At its best, dating is fun. At its worst, it's a nightmare. The secret to making dating fun is to release your expectations. As if *that's* an easy task! Perhaps this ritual will help.

Put a stopper in the sink and as you are getting ready for your date, go ahead and focus on all of your expectations. Visualize each expectation as a rock that could weigh down your evening, then imagine putting that rock into the sink.

I hope he's tall.
I want her to be beautiful.
I hope he doesn't talk about his job all night.
If she starts talking about her ex, I'm out of there.
If he doesn't like children, I'm in trouble.
I want her to like baseball.
I wonder if he's the marrying kind?
It would be nice if she offers to split the check.
It would be great if he notices my new haircut.
Will she be happy with the movie I picked out?

The list could get very long, very fast, and I'm only touching here on the surface stuff. Get as detailed as you like. Go ahead and admit your deep and dark fears. It just may free you from them. Eventually the sink will be full of your expectations. The last thing you need to do before you leave or before your date is due to pick you up is to pull the stopper on the sink. Wash your hands and visualize the soap dissolving all those rock-hard expectations. Smile, maybe even laugh, at the absurd notion that another person could exactly match what you want in a mate. As you wash your hands and as the soapy water flows down the drain, say:

> *I release my expectations of this evening (or afternoon) and I am clean and open to whatever happens.*

Since people rarely live up to another's expectations, you'll find yourself more relaxed and accepting and will probably have a better time because of it. Compatibility is more a matter of acceptance and less a matter of perfection. Enjoy your date.

New Lover

After the two of you have been dating a while you will eventually come to a very important decision: the decision to take the relationship to a higher level. This big step will need a lot of emotional preparation. Sexual intercourse changes a relationship and it is an important step toward a long-lasting commitment. Intimacy takes a long time to develop and sex brings us closer to one another more than any other bond, except perhaps motherhood. Of course to get to motherhood . . . Oh, well. It's the old question, which came first—the chicken or the egg? This ritual should be determined by what turns you on rather than on anything that I might suggest, but maybe some of my ideas will spark some of your own. Some people want to surprise their partners while others would rather discuss and plan for the big night, so I'll provide suggestions for both. Whichever way you decide, make sure you have protection from sexually transmitted diseases (STDs) or an unwanted pregnancy.

Prepare yourself by bathing, of course, but also by shaving, putting cologne in strategic places, putting on your sexiest underthings, and generally making yourself more alluring. If possible, have a spa day and let others pamper you. If the two of you have decided together that tonight's the night, you could share that spa day. What a delicious way to anticipate the evening's activities. During preparations, consciously think to yourself or say aloud:

Tonight, I open myself up to love and invite
[name] *into my heart and soul.*

The Surprise Approach

If you have chosen the surprise approach, you can make it more exciting by dropping subtle hints for a couple of days before. On the big day, have a plan of action. Here are some possibilities.

- Excuse yourself to go to the bathroom and return wearing something sexy. Lingerie goes a long way in conveying your intentions.
- During a kiss, whisper in your lover's ear: "I want you, right now." Sometimes there's nothing like the direct approach.
- If you prefer something a little less direct, gently encourage your lover's hands to explore new areas. Believe me, nature *will* take its course.

Be creative, but remember that with the surprise approach there is always a possibility of rejection. Be as sure as you can be before then, because having hurt feelings is not the way to end the evening. A surprise like this has to be carefully considered, and not everyone likes this kind of surprise—so be sure to take your potential lover's temperament into account. Good luck!

The Planned Rendezvous

Choose a place. It could be her place, his place, or someplace more neutral, like a hotel. I wouldn't recommend the car. At least not until you get to know one another a little better. If one of you has kids, go to the other's place. If you both have children, arrange for them to spend the night someplace else or go to a hotel. Nothing can ruin a romantic evening faster than the kids coming home from the movies early. It is better if they, or the two of you, are out for the night.

Set the mood—candles, music, clean sheets, and lots of pillows are the basics if you are a romantic. Make sure that you both like the music that's playing. Don't limit yourself to ballads either. If you are both hard-rock fans, by all means put on your favorite band. The first time my husband and I made love, it was to Santana's *Abraxis*. Hardly soothing, but it was exciting! That's what counts.

The first time with someone new can put an enormous amount of pressure on the two of you, so try to do something that is both relaxing and stimulating. A gentle back massage effortlessly translates into something more erotic. A glass or two of wine is a good relaxer, just don't overdo it or you may find certain things don't work too well.

Having lotions, towels, snacks, and cool drinks close by are also good ideas. I'm always hungry and thirsty after making love and this avoids the glaring light from the fridge. Besides, you can stay in your lover's arms after and savor the moment longer if certain necessities are within reach.

No matter what the two of you cook up, have fun and remember, this is only the beginning. Just like with dating, don't try to have too many expectations or you may end up being disappointed. Just go with the flow. Try to keep in mind that you are both going to be nervous. This will pass with time and experience. Tell your lover what excites you, and enjoy each other. Take your time and delight in the experience.

Decision to Live Together

The decision to live together is major. One interesting thing about this decision is that it is usually made after you've already been spending large chunks of time at your lover's place. The conversation usually goes something like this: "Why are we paying rent on two places, when I'm *here* most of the time?" Or, "I sure have an expensive closet halfway across town, with its own kitchen and bathroom." Or even, "Could you clean out a little bit more of the medicine cabinet for me?" Of course, it could be as simple as, "Let's move in together."

So, whether one of you is moving into the other's place or you are looking for a bigger place for the two of you, this ritual will help smooth the transition.

This ritual is done in the kitchen, the heart of the home. If one of you is moving into the other's place, do this ritual in the kitchen of the place where you both will be living. If you are moving into a new place, wait until you move in and do it in the kitchen of your new place.

It's best if you buy a new pot for this ritual; split the cost of this new pot as you will be splitting the costs of your new lives together. Next, find a recipe that you both love. It could be as simple as a jar of prepared pasta sauce or as complex as a complicated old family recipe for gumbo. If one of you provides the recipe, the other should provide the pot. If you both have a recipe for killer beef stew, split everything— including the recipe.

Pick a night that you know will be uninterrupted. Turn off the cell phone and ignore the doorbell. Don't check your e-mail and let the answering machine pick up the home phone. This is a night for love.

"The way to a man's heart is through his stomach," so the saying goes. Well, it's the same roadmap for a woman, too. Sharing food has a long history of being about friendship and compatibility. In ancient times, it was a sign of total trust to sit down at someone else's table and share food. It was also a sign of great respect to cook for someone, because you could very well be putting your last bit of grain on the table.

To live together in harmony is to combine all of these attributes: friendship, compatibility, trust, and respect. As you cook your meal mix all these ingredients into the pot, along with the carrots and the onions. Take turns stirring. Use both recipes. If neither one of you cooks from scratch, then take turns pouring something prepared into the pot. The fire beneath the pot represents the love that pulls it all together.

Enjoy your meal in romantic candlelight and celebrate the decision to be together. Leave the dishes until the next day, and make love after the meal to cement your bond.

Decision to Have Children

Deciding to start a family is one of the most profound moments in life. So why is this decision typically left to fate? Why is there no specific date set to begin this miraculous journey? The decision to have children is the most fortuitous time to begin the celebrations that will ultimately follow. Once the pregnancy happens the announcements and baby showers will be just a few of the joyous moments to look forward to. Then comes the actual birth of your child and all the activities, religious and otherwise, that follow that blessed event. Before this whirlwind begins, take a few moments to perform the following ritual, meant for the time when the two of you decide to bring another life into your hearts and your home.

Face each other in what will eventually be your child's room and grasp each other's hands. The following words will fill the space between you and provide a warm and cozy nest of welcoming wishes for your new child.

From the practical (passing on the family name) to the spiritual (raising another with your religious and moral beliefs) tell each other all the reasons you can think of for wanting a child of your own.

Next, say aloud all that you want to give a child. In addition to the practical considerations of a home and education, include the emotional and spiritual gifts you wish to bestow as well. Let this be a spontaneous expression of love and have fun with it. Take turns. Here are some possibilities:

I hope he has your sense of humor.
I want her to have your nose.
I hope he's tall like you.
I hope she has your soft skin.

When you have exhausted the possibilities, open the circle by letting go of your hands on one side. You are symbolically making room for the child to grasp them. Reveal the emotional nest to the soul of your child yet to be. Face the door and say the following:

We open our arms as we open our hearts to a new life.
Be welcome in this space as you are welcome in this
*   home.*
Take our open hands and complete this circle of love.

Place the first toy or piece of furniture into the room, then make love in this space. Keep in mind all that has just been spoken and felt as you create this new life.

Pregnancy

After you announce to the world that you are pregnant there are so many activities and celebrations—baby showers, buying furniture, decorating the nursery. But what about before you make that announcement? The day you and your spouse find out is thrilling and exciting, but it commonly has no associated rituals. This ritual celebrates the new life you will be bringing into the world. It is a private celebration for just the three of you and it is to be done before you share your news with family and friends.

Find a quiet place for both adults to sit comfortably. With both sets of hands on the belly of the mother-to-be, say the following words, but don't limit yourself to them alone. You are welcoming your child, so add whatever feels appropriate in the moment. Take turns and speak what is in your heart.

Welcome to life, little one. You are loved and wanted.
May your feet never stumble on the path of life.
May your hands be always full of what your heart
*   desires.*

May you be strong in body, mind, and spirit.
May your trials teach you the ways of living.
May your heartaches be few in number.
May your life be rich in family, friends, and
    happiness.
We await your birth with great anticipation.
We wish for you all the joy you are bringing to us.

Celebrate your pregnancy with a romantic dinner and place an extra plate and glass at the table to symbolically welcome your new bundle of joy.

Bringing Home Baby

There is usually a big fuss the day you bring home your new baby—pictures, video, family, and friends. But when the uproar dies down, you are left with just the three of you. The excitement of the day has dimmed and exhaustion sets in, but it's a good kind of tired—a joyful kind of tired. This short ritual is for that first time in your own home with only your partner and your baby. It's quiet and peaceful (at least until feeding time). Before you collapse into bed, take a little time for this ritual.

With the baby in the nursery, take stock of the room and imagine the changes it will undergo as your baby turns into a toddler. With your partner, discuss what these changes will be. Picture the change that will take place in the toys in the room. They will change from simple objects to catch the baby's eye to toys that stimulate your toddler's mind and help develop his coordination.

The next changes will take place when your child begins school. The crib will be gone and there will be a real bed in its place. The toys in the room will be even more advanced. Where stuffed animals used to sit on the shelves there are now books.

Jump forward a few more years to preteen. Your child's individual interests and tastes will now come to the forefront. Sports posters or horse statuettes could be the decorations of choice. Your child will begin to show his independence and will want to have a say in the décor of the room, even if you don't particularly like his choices.

Then, the teenage years set in. Rock posters will probably adorn the walls. A telephone in the corner and a Do Not Disturb sign on the door will represent your teenager's attitude. You probably will not be able to see the floor for months at a time, which might make you wonder if your hand would be safe if you dared to stick it under the bed.

Eventually the mess will go away as your child matures and you will find yourself feeling the tug on your heart that tells you your child will be leaving you in a few short years.

The final transformation will occur in the room when your child is finally out on his own. You will find yourself wandering into the room that will be empty of the presence of your child. At this point look at your baby and make a vow to not let the time go by too fast. Promise yourself to enjoy every minute of your child's life, even the hard times, for they will be gone in a flash.

Now, get some sleep. You're gonna need it.

Decision Not to Have Any *More* Children

Do this ritual when your family is just the right size for you, which may mean one, two, or ten children. Whether you are a single parent or a couple, this ritual includes your kids. If they are teenagers, I'm sure there will be much grumbling and rolling of eyes, but it really is best if all family members are present. This is a quickie, so assure everyone that you only need ten minutes of their time. It will also show children that have been begging for a little brother or sister that *that* possibility is *not* going to happen.

Gather in the room where most family members convene. In some houses that's the family room, but in others it's the game room, den, or even the kitchen. Once everyone is present, form a circle, but don't join hands. For a single-parent household, the following should be spoken by the parent. In a two-parent household, the partners should switch back and forth.

> *We gather to affirm that this family is complete.*
> *We gather to show our love for one another.*
> *We are bound in a circle of love.*
> *We are a family.*
> *There will be no more children until the next*
>   *generation.*
> *At that time, we will open our arms and welcome*
>   *them into this . . .*
> *Our family.*

Join hands as you say the final line. At this point, share your favorite memories associated with the birth of each child. Tell each child how special and how important he or she is in the family. Encourage them to share their favorite memories of siblings and parents alike. Have a giant group hug. The ritual, and your family, is complete.

Decision to *Not* Have Children

It's pretty much a given in today's society that when you grow up you get married. The next logical step must be to have children, but that is not necessarily right for everyone. Some people do not want children of their own, and the reasons don't really matter except to those individuals. I was lucky; when I met my husband I had already decided not to have children and he didn't want any more (he had two from a previous marriage). A child is a seven-day-a-week, twenty-four-hour-a-day responsibility that lasts a lifetime. There are those who simply do not want to take on that great a responsibility, and it's not for everyone. I've been with my husband for fifteen years and sometimes I'm still asked when we are going to have children. As much as we would prefer it not to be this way, *not* wanting children is considered an aberration in our society. This ritual is for those who make a conscious decision to *not* have children. Since the decision is a highly personal one (even if shared by your mate), this ritual should be done alone.

Find someplace where you can be alone and undisturbed for a while. Now think about all of society's reasons for having children. Then "answer" them for yourself. My suggestion would be to write down your answers to make them more concrete in your mind. If that makes you uncomfortable, then speak them aloud. At least have a list of questions so you don't forget something you think is important. The following is by no means a comprehensive list, but it will help you get started. I have also included some possible responses or ideas to think about.

Mother Culture whispers in our ears:

- *You're just being selfish.* That's a real possibility, but there shouldn't be anything wrong with that. I recently saw a great definition for selfishness that is highly appropriate to this situation. Being selfish is not about doing what *you* want, it is expecting *other people* to do what *you* want.

- *You'll regret this decision later in life.* This is also a possibility, but we all have regrets in life.

- *What's wrong, don't you like children?* This argument simply doesn't apply. Most people I know that have made a conscious decision to remain childless actually love children and are very good with other people's children. One woman I know runs a day care center and another is a teacher. Not wanting children of your own does not automatically translate into hating children.

- *There must be something wrong with you.* It takes a brave person to go against society's "norms," and those who do are typically considered "off" in some way.

- *The highest expression of love is a child.* This is strictly a matter of opinion.

- *Who will carry on your family name?* This is important only to a limited few and is usually only considered if the family is well known.

- *Do you want your bloodline to fade away?* Again, this tends to be important only to a certain segment of society.

- *Don't you want to be remembered and leave a part of yourself behind?* If you want to make a contribution to society, you can do that through works instead of through children.

- *You'll change your mind, and then it will be too late.* If you do change your mind later in life, there are always options. If you are past childbearing age, you could adopt. If you don't want to adopt, you can still make a positive difference in a child's life without becoming a parent. You could volunteer as a Big Brother or a Big Sister or for a host of other programs that need mentors for kids.

- *You will be lonely in your old age.* I'm sure friends and other family members will take care of that contingency.

- *Who will take care of you in your old age?* This should be something that you prepare and arrange for long before you require it. To be truly responsible is to be responsible for yourself. If you can't do that, how can you be responsible for a child?

This is a major decision in life and not one to be made lightly. But remember, it is your decision and your decision alone, whether you are male or female. If you are lucky enough to find a mate who agrees with you, all the better. If you are willing to go this far, the final part of this ritual *can* be sterilization. Be *sure* though if you want to carry it that far. Enjoy the rest of your life—child-free.

Milestone Birthdays

What are milestone birthdays? you may ask. These are the birthdays that have specific meaning in our society and culture. This ritual is designed for adult milestones, the decade birthdays (30, 40, 50, 60). When we reach a decade mark we have a tendency to be introspective and examine our lives. Past, present, and future are of major concern during these particular birthday celebrations. With that in mind, I offer this ritual.

Before your birthday, take your time and make several lists. You will be doing very specific things with these lists on the actual anniversary of the day of your birth. Start them several weeks or even months before your birthday. You could even begin making them the day after your birthday the year before. The first three lists are keepers, so a blank book would be a good place to write them, but make sure that past, present, and future are all on separate pages.

The Past

One of the reasons milestone birthdays can be depressing is because we tend to look to the past with regrets. Instead of doing that, make a list of all you have accomplished in your life to date. Along with the big accomplishments (house purchase, successful marriage, well-adjusted children, college degree) include the small ones as well (learning to swim, overcoming a fear of spiders, growing healthy houseplants). Be as specific or as general as you like. As you make this list, the accomplishments will grow and one memory will beget another. Think of this list as a depression lifter to read *any-time* you're feeling low, not just on your birthday.

The Present

Your next list is where you are now. Focus on the positives (we *will* get to the negatives later). What do you have in your life now that you enjoy and cherish? A great circle of friends? A job you love? Contentment in your home life? Where you live? Date this page with the day of your milestone birthday so that you can look back and see exactly where you were and what you were doing when you turned the age you are now.

The Future

Next, write your goals for the next ten years. Write each goal on a separate page, for you *may* be ripping them out some-time in the future. No life is perfect and we all have a few ripped pages, which brings me to the last list. . . .

Regrets

There are many people out there who will tell you that you should never regret the choices you have made in life. To them I say, baloney! We're only human—and regrets are part of life. One of my goals was to have a private pilot's license by the time I was forty. Well, it didn't happen for a variety of reasons. I made different choices, but sometimes I still regret that I didn't push hard enough for that one. But, as the famous saying goes: "You can have *any*thing you want, you just can't have *every*thing you want." I believe this becomes especially true as we get older and find ourselves giving up some of the goals we have set for ourselves. The reasons why matter less than the fact that you have given them up. It is important also that you have recognized that some goals are simply not attainable.

On this list, on loose paper, write the things that you *didn't* do and wanted to by this birthday. If you want to reset that goal, do so under Future and do not include it here. If, however, you've decided to give it up (flying, for me) write it on this list. This list is also for that date you turned down with that nerdy guy who turned out to be handsome and rich later in life. Anything in that vein is appropriate.

The Big Day

On the day of your birthday, reread all the above lists before your party or birthday cake. If you have neither a party nor a cake, then have at least one white candle handy. As you read Past, Present, and Future, light the candles or candle and toast your successes. You can choose to share any or all of these lists with family and friends. Or you can keep them to yourself. That is entirely up to you. Before blowing out the candles, take the Regrets list and light it from your birthday candles. Make sure you have a fireplace or fireproof container handy in order to let it burn (a glass baking dish works well). Now all your goals can extinguish your regrets! Since you've already made your wishes (the Future list), blow out your candles. Happy birthday!

Divorce—Breakup—Loss of Friendship

It is never a happy occasion when a relationship ends, no matter what the reason. Divorce is final and you have a piece of paper that proves it, but when you break up with someone there is no paperwork. That can invoke a feeling of loss but without the sense of closure that the courts provide. The same can be said for the loss of a friend, whether the two of you drifted apart over a long period or one simply said, "I no longer want to have anything to do with you." After the initial hurt, we go through many stages to get over it. A loss is a loss, and I'm not a psychologist; however, I have used this ritual for myself, and it does help to put the loss of a friend or lover in concrete terms.

You will need a thick piece of biodegradable rope (something large enough to write on), a sharp knife or scissors, and a marker.

We've all heard the term "tying the knot." This ritual— literally—*unties* the knot. But first it has to be tied.

Take the rope and write your name on one end. On the other end write the name of the person who is no longer a part of your life. Now, tie a knot in the middle. As you hold on to the knot, think of all the *good* times in the relationship. Go through old photo albums and reread old love letters. Relive the happy memories the two of you have shared. This can take a while, possibly even all day or over a weekend. Try to keep your mind off of fights and unhappy memories. If you find yourself crying, that's okay. Keep the rope with you while you are doing this.

When you are finished, go to a favorite spot the two of you shared. Again, it needs to be a place with happy associations. It could be a park bench, the beach, or a favorite hiking trail. Sit there for a while and focus on the specific reasons the two of you are no longer together. Try to come to a better understanding of the underlying causes of the breakup. Once you have a firm grip on those reasons, untie the knot, cut the rope in two, and say:

> *I release you with love and hope for you only*
>   *the best in life.*
> *Good-bye.*

Tie both ropes around separate bench legs or trees or whatever feels most appropriate. You are now separate but still share the same space. You are symbolically leaving the relationship behind as you turn and leave this place that was special to the two of you. It is my hope that whenever you visit there in the future, even after the ropes are gone, you will remember only the good times of your relationship.

Note: You are leaving your half of the rope also, because you are no longer the person you were in that relationship. Reinvent yourself and create new ties.

Parent(s) Moving In

There comes a time when our parents can no longer live on their own. Be it for economic, physical, or emotional reasons, it becomes time for the children to care for the parents who once cared for them. This is an extremely difficult time and requires major adjustments by everyone in the family, even those who do not live in the same house. The psychological ramifications are deep seated and can be hard to overcome. If you find yourself in this situation, I highly recommend speaking to a family therapist before the first box is packed. This ritual is not intended to address the complex issues involved when a parent moves in; it is simply a welcoming ritual to help your parent(s) feel like a part of the household instead of an appendage to it.

This is a ritual for the whole family. You will need a large piece of poster board, colored pens or pencils, crayons, stickers, glitter—basically whatever you can think of to decorate the poster board.

Before the new family member moves in, gather the rest of the household together. Fold the poster board in half and create a program like you would see for a play. On the outside, write "The Smith Family's Adventures," or "All my Joneses," or "Fun with Dick, Jane, Harry, and Sally." You will, of course, use your own names.

On the inside, create a cast list. Be creative here and describe your "duties" in the household. It will give your newest member an idea of what everyone does in the house. For example:

- *Richard*—Husband Extraordinaire, Father of the Year, Fixer of Leaky Plumbing

- *Janet*—Wise Wife, Mender of Broken Hearts, Seamstress to the Stars

- *Harry*—Dependable Son, Honor Roll Student, Trash Can Emptier

- *Sally*—Dutiful Daughter, Soccer Superstar, Fridge Cleaner

Next, add your parent(s). For example:

- And Introducing! *Sylvia*—Grandmother the Great, Garage Sale Hunter, Baker of Fabulous Desserts
- *Mark*—Grandfather of the Fabulous Two, Pun Master, Carver of the Thanksgiving Turkey

Now decorate the rest of the "program." Make it as elaborate and fun as possible. Have the program waiting on their bed the day they move in and then celebrate with a huge family dinner. Take it slow, and always remember to keep a sense of humor.

4

If Everybody Jumped off a Bridge, Would You, Too?

PARENTS AND CHILDREN

THIS CHAPTER describes the unique circumstances surrounding the raising of children. The first part deals with the early years of childhood, the years in which you are the one making all the decisions for your child. The rituals in this section, although important to the child at the time, will be the ones that you as a parent will remember for much longer. At this time *you* are more important to your child than anyone or anything else. You are the comfort, the unwavering support, and the guiding hand to your child. Here you'll find ways to celebrate all the firsts in a child's life, the firsts that the child won't likely remember later in life.

Then we move on to the rituals that you, as a parent, will hopefully love, but I can almost guarantee you that your teenager will probably view them as lame. It's entirely up to you how hard you want to push to do these rituals with your teenager. The good news? In our culture, most of these events are already surrounded by rituals.

Finally, the focus shifts to the most intense experiences for children: sex, divorce, remarriage. Most of these experiences have their own rituals for parents, but few for children. The rituals here are designed as an enhancement to the rituals already present for these life-changing events. No one ritual or talk is going to get you, as a parent, through these issues with your children, but these rituals will provide a starting point and perhaps help you generate additional solutions to some of the hardest parenting problems.

There are so many ways to celebrate a child's life every day. Whether you do these rituals together or separately, with or without your child's cooperation, you will find the memories even more precious because you took the time to make the event extra special.

First Word

A child typically speaks for the first time when you least expect it and never when you are trying to get her to speak. It happens at the dinner table or while you are watching a movie. At first, you aren't really sure it happened. You stop what you are doing and encourage your child to say the word(s) again. Once you are sure you have heard a meaningful word or more, the celebration begins—the phone calls to relatives, coaxing the words out of your child's mouth again and again. Beginning to use language, the primary way we communicate, is a huge leap for your child. Words play such an important part in our lives that we need a ritual to celebrate their first use. This ritual is designed as a precursor to the ritual "Learning to Read" (page 52).

* * *

The first word spoken by a child is typically one identifying mama or dada. Parents are the most important people in a young child's life and, although this will change as she walks the path toward maturity, words will gain more importance.

Buy a dictionary, preferably a big solid one that will last a long time, and write the child's name on the inside front cover. Follow that with the date of her first spoken word and what that word was. Reference the page number where that word can be found. Place this dictionary in a place in the child's room where she can see it but not reach it. It is to be used later, when she begins to read. For now she would probably only want to color the pages or see what the cover tastes like.

In the meantime, enjoy listening to your young one call you mama and dada.

First Step

It's breathtaking when your child takes his first step! What an amazing process preceded it. Little hands that grasped your fingertips loosened ever so slightly as your child became more confident. He pulled himself up on table and chair legs and held on to furniture as he made his way around the room. Finally, he let go and took his first step into a larger world. This signals the time when you are able to cushion every fall. He is learning (in baby steps, of course) to stand or fall on his own. With that in mind, I offer this ritual.

When a child is born, an imprint is often made of the baby's foot. I submit that after that first step is a good time to repeat the process. Instead of a birth certificate identification, you will be creating a reminder for your child of what walking is all about. This item will remind him to always move forward. A door to the world has just opened.

Get a big ink pad and a world map. Spread the map on the floor next to the ink pad. Help your toddler to step onto the ink pad and then to make tracks across the map. Write the child's full name and the date of that first step just below his footprints. After the ink dries, flip the map over and write famous quotes on the back. Include your favorites about moving forward in life. Here are a few of my favorites:

- "A journey of a thousand miles begins with a single step."   —Confucius
- "Do not criticize a man until you have walked a mile in his shoes."   —Unknown
- "Two roads diverged in a wood and I—I took the one less traveled by, and that has made all of the difference." —Robert Frost
- "One small step for man, one giant leap for mankind."   —Neil Armstrong
- "Advance confidently in the direction of your dreams, endeavor to lead the life you have imagined, and you will meet with a success unexpected in common hours."   —Henry David Thoreau
- "Let him who would move the world first move himself."   —Socrates
- "Do not walk in front of me, I may not follow. Do not walk behind me, I may not lead. Just walk beside me and be my friend."   —Albert Camus

- "The rewards of the journey far outweigh the risk of leaving the harbor."   —Unknown
- "I'm a slow walker, but I never walk back." —Abraham Lincoln

After writing the quotes on the back, roll up the map and put it someplace safe. As a parent, you may wish to take it out and look at it as your child grows. When it is time for your child to leave home permanently, present him with this map as a guide to the world and remind them that the world is his to travel across. The little footprints prove it.

First Haircut

Talk about scary! Someone coming at you with a pair of scissors, something Mommy always told you not to play with. A stranger touching your hair with tools that make noise! Getting that first haircut can be traumatic for your child. This ritual should help ease your child's fears.

First of all, try to take your child with you a couple of times when you get your hair cut. You know he will probably get bored, so bring along a favorite toy or coloring book. It's important to show your child that this is something Mommy and Daddy do all the time. This will help him be at ease when it's their turn.

Point out to the child that even lawns get haircuts. Take him outside when the lawn is getting mowed so he can see that it doesn't hurt the grass to cut it, it actually makes it look nicer. Bend down with him and touch the grass, both before and after it's mowed, to show him how different it feels.

After you go back inside, if you have them, get out all the implements that will be used to cut your child's hair, including electric trimmers. Show your child how each item works and what kind of noise it makes. If the sound of the electric trimmer frightens your child, remind him of the lawn mower and the sound it made. Point out that the trimmers aren't nearly that loud.

Children are great believers in magic, so when your child is in the barber chair, tell him that the smock or towel will protect him and keep him safe. Keep telling him that there is nothing to be afraid of. Remind him that he saw Mommy or Daddy getting a haircut and that it didn't hurt. Take a photo of him in the barber's chair and tell him how special he is and what a big boy he is. Tell him that he looks just like Daddy sitting in the big chair.

When the haircut starts, remind him again that his hair is getting trimmed just like the grass got cut. Remember to save a lock of hair and store it with the photo as a remembrance for him when he gets older.

After the cut, take your child out for a special treat like an ice cream cone or an hour in the park. You want to show him how proud you are that he was such a good little boy. The next time shouldn't be quite so traumatic.

Show off your child's stunning new look.

Learning to Read

Reading is one of the most important skills your child can have. It is the basis of much learning. (One can also learn through experience, of course, and in some circumstances, experience is the best teacher.) Do this ritual when you decide that you are going to begin teaching your child to read.

The day you begin teaching your child to read, celebrate by taking her to the nearest library or bookstore. Walk with her through the stacks and explain that all these books will soon be open to her. Let her know that she can explore the world through reading books. She can visit exotic ports of call during any period in history just by reading about them. Instruct her to use books in order to learn anything she wants to know, from how to build a paper airplane to how to fly a jumbo jet. Tell her she can read about places that don't really exist except in the pages of fiction, from cities built in the clouds to worlds in distant galaxies. Do this often as your child learns to read, and watch her embrace all that books can provide her.

As your child grows, take that dictionary that you bought her when she said her first word and show her her name and that word. Explain to her that this book contains all the other ones in it and if she doesn't understand what a word means that she read in a book, she can ask for help in looking it up. As she learns to read, open the dictionary at random at least once a month. Once a week would be even better. Choose a word from the page that you do not know and teach it to your child. Have her try to use this word as much as possible during the next week. You may find that you have to correct her usage from time to time. By the time your child can do this on her own, she will probably have a vocabulary larger then most kids her age. As a matter of fact, her vocabulary could very easily overcome yours if you are not careful.

Encourage your child to do this ritual throughout her life and she will always be learning.

Happy reading!

First Tooth Lost

Your child will typically lose a baby tooth at about the same time he starts kindergarten, at about the same time he is starting to realize that there is more to life than home and family. Losing that first baby tooth is often scary. The loose tooth wiggles and you can push it around with your tongue, loosening it even more. Your child may be afraid of removing it, for it might hurt. When it does finally come out, with or without help, there should be a celebration. This ritual precedes the tooth fairy, but has some similarities. Exchanging something small for something larger is the theme here, just as your child begins to put away the small things from babyhood for the larger ones of childhood.

Have your child pick an item from his room that to *him* is now babyish—a toy, a favorite blanket, a stuffed animal, or even a cherished piece of clothing that no longer fits. It may take some cajoling from you to get him to make a decision. Explain to the child that this item, along with his tooth, will be going away forever. Tell him that he is no longer a baby and now that he has lost his first baby tooth, it's time to start giving up other things of a babyish nature.

At bedtime, place the tooth under the pillow for the tooth fairy and have the chosen item near by. Replace the tooth with whatever is traditional to you, be it money or something else. Replace the favorite "baby" item with something that is comparable but more "grown-up." Make it something that requires a little more thought and concentration. You might even go one step beyond where your child is now and give him something that he can grow into.

When he wakes, take some time to praise him for putting away baby things and tell him how proud you are that he is getting older.

First Adult Tooth

Inevitably, shortly after the loss of your child's first baby tooth, the adult tooth becomes visible and starts to push through. This is also a big deal for your child, for although the previous section is about loss, this event is about gain and growth. This ritual is one that will continue for some time and needs a bit of advance preparation.

Gather together a cup you can write on, a marker, a knife, toothpicks, and an avocado. Other fruits that have pits, such as plums or peaches, can be used as well. You will get the best results, however, with an avocado. You will also need a small pot and soil. Buy a pot that can also be marked on or decorated. (A clay pot is great for this ritual, because decorating kits are available that are designed specifically to be used with terra cotta.)

Sit down with your child and explain that the avocado is like babyhood and inside the avocado is the seed of adulthood. Help your child to cut the avocado in half and pull out the seed. Explain that the seed, like her new tooth, will grow, but only with the proper care. Have her write her name on the cup. Take the time to decorate the pot now, as well, even though you won't be using it for a while yet. Fill the cup with water and stick toothpicks all around the avocado seed. The toothpicks should rest on the rim of the cup and the lower half of the seed should be in the water. Place it in a sunny window.

Tell your child that she will be responsible for taking care of the seed so it will grow. Tell her that she must take care of her tooth also, so *it* will grow. Encourage her to check the water level in the cup and make sure the lower end of the seed is always in the water. Correspond this activity to teeth brushing. If she checks the water every time she brushes her teeth, the seed will never dry out and it will eventually grow into a plant. This does two things, it instills a sense of responsibility for another living thing in her and at the same time encourages good dental hygiene. Let her know that she must check the water level every morning and night.

When the seed begins to sprout, tell your child that she is becoming a big girl, just like the seed is becoming a plant.

After a good root system has been established and leaves begin shooting out the top, plant the seed in the pot with the soil. By this time, your child's tooth should be well on its way to being in. Encourage your child to continue to take care of the plant, and with care it will grow into a full and healthy plant, just like she will eventually have a full set of adult teeth.

Happy growing!

First Day of School

The first day of school can be another one of those traumatic events. But this one is often just as traumatic for the parents as it is for the child. Releasing a child into the world, where others will begin to have significant influence, can be terrifying for a parent. Knowing that little Janie or Johnnie will bring home new words, ideas, and values should be exciting and fun, for all involved. This ritual makes the first day of school into an adventure for the child and a release for the parents.

There is always a list of school supplies that need to be gathered together before the first day of school. While you are at the store buying the items your child will need, there is something else you need to buy: an inexpensive apron.

The day before the first day of school, hide all the school supplies throughout the house. Place each item in a separate location, but easy enough for the child to find. Next, make a map with an X marking where each item is hidden. Accompany each item with a smaller map showing the location of the next one. Accompany the last item with a "treasure map" leading to the school. Label the school as the biggest treasure of all. You could even draw a treasure chest with the name of the school on the outside of it.

You can make the treasure hunt elaborate if you wish. The family can dress up like pirates or safari hunters. Have fun with this. You are teaching your child something she will carry with her the rest of her life—learning is an adventure to look forward to.

Before the hunt, tie the scissors to the apron and put it on. Before you give your child the first map, tell her that she is going to start a great adventure the next day, but before she can go on that treasure hunt, she must find all the tools she will need. Inform her that she must do this on her own. Tie one of the apron strings to the child's wrist and tell her that her parents will always be waiting at home for her, but that this adventure is for her alone. Then help your child cut that string that connects you. Tell her that she can take that string with her and it will always remind her that her parents love her and are never very far away.

Give your child the first map. During the hunt, keep affirming how much fun this is and how much fun school's going to be. It will be at least as much fun as this, maybe more. Praise her every time she finds an item. After everything is found and put together in her backpack, take the string from around her wrist and tie it to one of the straps.

The next morning when you drop her off at school, tell her if she gets sad or lonely to look at the string and think of her parents. Try not to cry in front of your child. It will only upset her. Tell her you can't wait to hear about her great adventure. Let her know, one last time, that the treasures she will find in school are new friends, fun, and learning.

Send her on her way and try not to shed too many tears on the way to work or back home. Just think of all the new and wonderful things that you will be able to talk about when your child gets home.

Congratulations, your child is now a part of a larger world.

School Year Beginning/Ending

The beginning and the ending of the school year are transitional times for both parents and kids, and your children rarely see them the same way you do. Ah, to be a kid again and look forward to a whole season without school. For parents, the approaching summer combines the joy of upcoming vacations with the issues of child care. In the Fall, the issues shift to the reestablishment of routines and the return of homework. These rituals will help ease that transition and make you and your child more aware of the time that is approaching. Begin the rituals approximately a week before each event.

Starting the School Year

Before beginning the year there will be the obligatory shopping for school supplies. Sometimes the back-to-school shopping includes purchasing clothing and other personal items, such as backpacks, new sneakers, and such. After each trip, place all the new items in the same room (a corner of the dining room might work well). Make sure it's a space where the things can be left untouched until school actually begins. Displaying the clothes and supplies in this way should make your child excited about wearing or using them. That way they will look forward to the first day of school with enthusiasm instead of dread.

Out of cardboard or poster board make a doorway that sits in front of these items. To encourage your child to look forward to returning to school, the doorway should be decorated with the child's new grade, school name, friends that will be in the same class, and favorite teachers or activities that the child does not participate in during the summer. This display will also be helpful to you in focusing on what you need to do to prepare your child, in turn, preparing yourself, too.

The weekend before the first day of school, walk through this doorway and organize the supplies and clothes and take them to your child's room. Pick out the outfit for the first day and let your own excitement show.

On the morning of the first day, move the cardboard doorway to stand over the doorway that your child will leave through in order to get to school.

The year has begun.

Ending the School Year

For the end of the school year, you will be doing the same thing except that this time the doorway will be decorated with the images of summer—pool parties, camp, baseball, skateboarding.

Behind the doorway you will place those things of summer that your child is not allowed to use until school is out for the year. On the last day of school, place the summer doorway over the outside of the door your child will use when they come home.

Have fun and enjoy your summer!

Receiving Allowance

Teaching your child about money can begin in the simplest ways: first, by guiding her to save gifts of money or to spend those gifts on something she desires. But the best way to teach your child responsible money management is by giving her an allowance. Usually an allowance is a fair exchange: the child must perform duties in exchange for money. Taking out the trash, vacuuming the living room, or mowing the yard are all ways in which to earn an allowance. Lunch money is not the same as an allowance, although managing lunch money can also be a learning experience, but that is money set aside for a specific purpose (or it's supposed to be) and it is not covered in this ritual. This ritual is for money that the child decides what to do with.

Set up a system of responsibilities and compensation that you think is fair and present it to your child. You could even have a chart, similar to a menu—that has the dollar amount for each chore. Or you could have a set amount for a set number of chores. How you present this to your child is entirely up to you.

Have five large envelopes ready when you give your child her first allowance. Break down the money and give it to her in small increments. For example, if her weekly allowance is $10 give her ten singles. If it's a monthly allowance break it down into $5's and $1's. Explain to your child that from now on she will need to save money for the things she wants. A child's wish list is usually very long, so have her figure out the top three things that she wants most, anything from a new video game cartridge to a pretty hair ornament. It could even be as substantial as a TV or phone for her room.

Have your child write the name of each item on the front of a different envelope and explain to her that if she wants these things then she must save for them. Tell her that it will probably take some time. She can decorate the front of the envelopes with photos of the longed-for item in addition to writing the name of it on the outside.

The fourth envelope is for the little things that come up, like an ice cream cone after school, a slice of pizza with friends, or a favorite video rental, or to supplement her lunch money so she can have a dessert on a day when lunch money wouldn't normally cover that extravagance.

The fifth and final envelope is for a large purchase sometime in the future. Label this envelope "long-term investment." At least a dollar out of every allowance must go into this envelope and the parent and the child will decide together what it will be used for. It could be for a car, college tuition, a trip to Europe one summer, or a winter ski trip with friends. This is a simple way to teach your child about saving. *You* will keep this envelope in a safe place. The other envelopes will be kept in your child's possession, in her room.

Within each envelope, place a dollar that is not their allowance, but comes from you. Explain that this is seed money and must *never* be removed, for if they remove the seed the plant will never grow.

Congratulations, you've just set your child on a positive financial path for the future.

First Sleepover

One of my favorite sayings designed to break the tension when someone thinks I am taking a subject too lightly (which usually means I think they are being way too serious) is to say, "Of course I am 'making fun.' Do you think fun just happens? No, we must 'make' fun." The expectations a child has about his first sleepover is that fun will just happen. This ritual is to encourage your child to "make fun" instead. Maybe that way he will stay all night, instead of calling you at 10 P.M. (or earlier), wanting to come home.

* * *

While you are helping your child pack, tell him that with every piece of clothing he is packing, he is packing your love also. Encourage him to take his own pillow and let him know that when he squeezes that pillow, he is squeezing you as well.

Along with his overnight bags, put together a "make fun" kit that he can take with him. It could be a shoebox or another small bag. But you won't fill it with toys or games. It is too easy for a favorite toy to get left behind or lost, and that would cause your child to be even more upset if he decided to come home. So instead of toys, fill the box or bag with *ideas* on how to "make fun." You could start out with some of the following suggestions:

- Ask the mom at the other house if you can make your own ice cream sundaes. Get creative with the toppings (peanut butter actually tastes good on ice cream).

- Pop popcorn. Have a contest to see who can get the most pieces in the other ones' mouths . . . from across the room. (This makes a mess, so be sure to ask permission first.)

- Hold a gumball in your mouth and try to drop it into a glass. (This is also messy, but a little paper around the glass should take care of the misses.)

- See who can stand on his head the longest.

Once you get going, your child will chime in with suggestions of his own. Write them all down on separate pieces of paper and put them in the "make fun" kit. When you drop your child off for his sleepover, remind him that his clothes hold your love, his pillow holds your hugs, and that he can "make fun" all he wants.

Happy sleepover, and sweet dreams to *you* knowing that *he* is having a good time!

Home Alone

It's a big step for both the parents and the child when the child is trusted to stay home by herself for the afternoon or evening. It reminds me of a quote I have always loved: "If we do not trust our children, how can we ever expect them to become trustworthy?" And it's not just about trust either, it is also about responsibility. Has she fed or walked the dog as needed? Has she finished homework before playing computer games or watching a favorite TV show? This ritual shows your child that you not only trust her to take care of the house, but that you respect her for doing so.

Responsibility, trust, respect—this ritual honors all three in your child. There is usually a list of do's and don'ts for a child staying home alone. For example:

Do . . .
- Keep the door locked.
- Finish your homework.
- Walk the dog.
- Feed the cat.
- Respect others' privacy. (This is a don't as well. "Don't go through dresser drawers.")

- Fix yourself dinner.
- Entertain yourself. (This can also have a *don'ts* corollary)

Don't . . .

- Tell anyone that you are home alone.
- Invite friends over (unless permission is given ahead of time).
- Eat a bunch of junk food.
- Let anyone in the house.
- Open the door for strangers.

You get the idea. Make your own list. Write it down on the back of an enlarged photo of the front of the house. Or you can draw a crude picture of the house and write the list on the back of that. Give this to your child and tell her that you are giving her the house for the night, but with that gift comes responsibilities. Show her the back of the picture and ask her to check off each item as it is done . . . or not done. Go out and have a good time.

When you get home, ask your child to get the list. If it's late in the evening, you will probably want to do this the next day. Have your child hold on to the list, then ask her if she did everything on the list and if she respected the don'ts. Of course, she is going to say yes and try to show you where she checked everything off. Don't take the list. Don't even look at it. Instead, tell her that you trust her if she says it is so.

Give her an assignment. Have her go look up the word *integrity*, then add your definition to the one she finds. Integrity is staying true to your word even when no one is watching. With a highlighter, have her write the word *integrity* over the list you left with her, Tell her to keep that list and use it every time she is left alone and as long as she honors her responsibilities, you will never ask to look at it. You don't expect her to be perfect in the future, but you do expect her to be forthcoming about things she missed or rules that weren't followed. You trust her and take her at her word, but the punishment will be much worse if you find out from someone else that she let her friends come over while you were gone, or broke some other rule.

If she has done something she wasn't supposed to, she at least has a visual reminder of that wrongdoing and her betrayal of your trust in the form of the list. Probably with these reminders, she won't do it again.

Enjoy the trust you are building with your child and let her prove that trust by going out more often.

Enjoy yourself.

First Meal Cooked

A recent study indicates, for the past century at least, that each successive generation cooks less than their parents did. In this society, we have fast food and moderate to expensive restaurants on just about every corner. Why cook when someone else can not only cook the meal, but clean up the mess as well? Sharing food has a long and ancient tradition of showing respect and honor for one another. It's not just about feeding your body but your spirit as well. This ritual teaches your child about those things, but also instills a sense of fun in food preparation.

* * *

When your child starts to show an interest in cooking, plan for a day when you can help him prepare his first dish. Make that dish something that can be fun and whimsical, like gingerbread persons or pancakes. Contrast this fun and whimsical dish with your best china and fancy cloth napkins when you set the table beforehand.

Decorate the food with happy faces or make animal shapes. Let your child choose which it will be. After everything is cooked, bring the serving dish to the table and have the whole family standing at the table, waiting for the food. You could even have some of your child's friends over, if you like, and make a real party out of it.

Now for the serious part (although I'm sure there will be some giggles along the way) have your child serve each person in turn. As he does so, have him say:

> *I respect you and show you love and friendship*
> *by preparing and sharing this food with you.*

In response, each person should say:

> *I accept your love and friendship and I honor*
> *and trust you by eating what you have prepared.*

During the meal, tell stories about ancient meals and how sharing food was a great honor, because food was not as abundant. Sharing food might mean there would be less for you and your family later on. Accepting food from someone else meant that you trusted that person not to poison you and steal your lands and goods. Explain that "breaking bread together" is a time-honored tradition and that learning to cook honors that tradition.

Congratulate your child and encourage him to continue to learn and honor others by cooking.

First Makeup Application

When a girl starts wearing makeup it is much different from simply playing with Mommy's lipstick. This is no longer dress-up, this is a girl trying to enhance her natural beauty. This is also a girl trying to fit in with her peers. And let's not forget, she is also trying to be attractive to the opposite sex. In the world of birds it's the males that show the most brilliant colors in order to attract a mate. With human beings it's the females. This ritual is a reminder of how beautiful natural beauty can be, but also how a little extra-added oomph can't hurt.

Mom, it's time to gather together some of your own makeup to experiment with. You will also need a teenage magazine or two as well as photos of some of the more colorful and exotic birds. Set aside a couple of hours with your daughter to teach her about proper skin care and how to apply makeup.

Go through the teen magazines and have your daughter cut out photos of women she finds beautiful. Have her cut out the photos of makeup that she thinks are extreme and would never wear as well. Pair these up with the photos of the birds. Cardinals for photos of those with dramatic red lipstick. Turtle doves for the more subtle shades of tan and brown. Parrots could be paired with the extreme or overdone faces. Staple or tape the bird photos with the face photos. After everything is paired up, spend the next couple of hours practicing applying makeup. Don't limit yourself to the tasteful. Try the tacky, too. Mom, you'll need to make up your face also, especially with the extreme applications. If nothing else it will show your daughter how ridiculous it can look on someone else. Make it fun.

If you have an instant or a digital camera, you can add photos of you and your daughter wearing various shades to the bird and magazine photos. When you're done, wash your faces and stand side by side in front of the mirror. Look for similarities in your features and reaffirm your daughter's natural beauty. Tell her that although you will accept her now wearing makeup that, to you, she is the *most* beautiful without it.

Have fun, get messy, but most of all, laugh.

First Shave

It's funny, some of the things that as an adult seem onerous are looked at as great by kids. Shaving is one of these. When a girl shaves her legs for the first time or a boy his face, it is an outward sign of physical maturity. They are thrilled that their bodies are starting to show that they are growing up. This short ritual is to help your child determine when this big step should take place and to celebrate it when it finally does occur.

We've all heard the term *peach fuzz* to describe hair that's starting to come in, but still isn't really ready for shaving. With that in mind, pick up a peach and a kiwi from the grocery store when your child starts talking about shaving. Ask your child to close his or her eyes and put out a hand for the peach. Have your child feel the fuzz, then feel his or her face or legs. Ask if it feels the same. If the answer is affirmative, tell your child it is not yet time to shave.

With your child's eyes still closed, take the peach away and hand over the kiwi. Say that when the hair begins to feel prickly like the kiwi, then it will be time for that first shave.

Do this ritual once a month until it is finally time for their first shave. When that time comes, pick out a nice new razor or an electric shaver and present it as a gift. You will want to teach your child how to use it, of course, and give him or her all the safety tips you can think of along with advice on what to do in the case of shaving nicks or cuts.

Afterward, celebrate with a nice peach pie or peach cobbler. As you eat it, let your child know that the pie represents a part of childhood that is now gone.

Keep it sharp and shave on!

First Dance

Most kids are nervous when it comes time to attend their first dance, and most of this nervousness stems from the unknown. They aren't sure what to expect except what they have heard from others. Those others are doing nothing to ease your child's fears. As is often the case with older kids, only the horror stories are shared. It's easier to focus on something that went wrong than on the fun that was had. This ritual will help you help your child overcome insecurities and attend that first dance with a feeling of preparedness instead of trepidation.

Sit down with your child about a week before the dance. This is best done by the parent of the opposite sex, because a lot of the nervousness involves interacting with the opposite sex in a social, instead of a school, atmosphere. Tell your child that you're going to rehearse for the dance, just like you would for a play. The biggest difference is that you, as the parent, are going to be your child and your child will play the other attendees of the dance. This is a round-about way to get your child to show you his or her fears and, at the same time, for you to suggest solutions to potentially embarrassing situations.

Start with how to ask or respond to the basics, like:

What's your name?
Aren't you in my (math, science, music) class?
Would you like to dance?
Can I get you a glass of punch?

Then segue to the tougher situations:

Being turned down
Being ignored
Someone making fun of what you are wearing
Someone making fun of how you dance

After this playacting you, as a parent, will have a deeper understanding of your child's insecurities. Always remember to maintain a sense of humor about the whole situation.

On the day of the dance, remind your child about the "rehearsal" you did together, and that if any discomfort arises, he or she should recall those answers that you came up with together. Compliment your child's appearance. This makes your child feel good and at least a little more courageous when he or she first walks into the dance.

As a parting shot, remind your child to have fun!

First Crush/Broken Heart

When your child hurts, so do you, and a broken heart is the one thing you can't fix. Band-Aids or kisses to make it better no longer work as your child begins to become familiar with a pain that is more adult in nature. Sometimes that pain occurs because she likes someone who doesn't like her. At other times, it's a breakup with a boyfriend. Try this ritual when your young one is experiencing her first broken heart.

Often, children don't want to talk to their parents when something like this happens. Try this to break the ice. Think of a favorite item that your child loved that was damaged in some way (for example, torn pages or broken spokes) and remind your child of how she felt when that happened. She will probably say, "That's different." Yes, that's true, but it still hurt. The pain is more intense now, because the item she lost then couldn't love her back—and a person can. Tell her that this pain, too, will go away in time, but that it will take longer to get over a broken heart than the loss of a "thing."

As a reminder, drive her to a store where that long-lost item can be found. Show her the shelves full of new items like the one that was lost or damaged and that she loved so much. Explain that there are that many people out there and that out of those, at least a few will return her love in the future. And that of all those, list all the people in her life that love her now, starting with yourself.

Over the next few weeks make a little extra effort to reaffirm that she is still loved and will be loved still more.

Becoming a Teenager

I saw this plaque in a friend's home the other day: "Raising teenagers is like nailing Jell-O to a tree." After I stopped laughing (which took a while), I realized that this was a perfect way to describe the inexplicable challenges to raising a teenager. Whether male or female, turning thirteen is a very big deal. In some cultures, this represents the age that one becomes an adult or takes on adult responsibilities for the first time. Society expects much more from a teenager than it does from a twelve-year-old. It doesn't matter that it's only one year's difference; at thirteen, the burdens of society begin to weigh more heavily upon young shoulders. Friends, family, and teachers no longer let the mistakes of childhood slide. A teenager is put in a pressure cooker and the heat is turned up. How teenagers react and cope with those extra pressures will determine what kind of adults they become. With that in mind, I offer the following ritual. Good luck, and get that nail gun out, the Jell-O is starting to congeal.

After whatever religious and cultural rituals have taken place concerning your child turning thirteen, take some time for a quiet talk. Explain to your child that you understand that he is changing and growing up. Tell him also that there will be occasions and situations over the next few years that will be difficult to talk about, especially with a parent. Stress to your child that he can tell you anything and that you truly do understand what he is going through and will be going through during the coming years.

After this talk, present your child with a blank book. This can be as simple as a composition notebook from the drugstore or as elaborate as an engraved leather-bound book. Say to your child, as you give him this gift (or, if speaking the words is too uncomfortable, write the following on the inside front cover along with the date and occasion):

> *For those times when it is too embarrassing or too painful to speak aloud, write your worries and cares here and know that, although I will not hear them, your words are held safe in this book. Know also that my love is in these pages and that with each thing you write upon them, my love is released to help ease your woes. When you cannot speak to me, find peace in expression by writing in these blank pages. After these pages are filled, I will provide you with another book, and another, for however long you need. Simply ask me.*

You have just provided your child with a nonjudgmental "friend" to act as a release valve for all his teenage pressures.

Starting High School

Starting high school is thrilling, no doubt, but it is also a big step. Your child is now entering the final years as a "kid." High school is where the social skills needed in life are honed and sharpened. *Everything* is a big deal in high school. So much happens for the first time. The intensity of events and the emotional responses to those events escalates. This ritual shows your budding young man or woman that, although swimming with the big fishes, he or she still has a long way to go.

Sometime during the summer before your child starts high school, take a short trip to your local aquarium. If a family vacation is in the offing, consider a trip to a place near the water that offers a view of marine life. The best way to approach this is with a sense of humor. If you are too serious, your child will most likely roll his eyes and tell you that he "knows" *everything* you are saying. Come to think of it, he will probably do that anyway. Oh, well.

Start talking about how the different fishes are like the kids in high school. There are the sharks. These are the bullies that will attack other fish just because it is their nature. Those other fish really don't deserve to be attacked or eaten, nor have they done anything wrong, it's just the way things are sometimes. There are angel fish, the really beautiful ones that seem too delicate to approach or touch, but are typically the most friendly. Then come the clown fish, flamboyant and always looking for attention and trying to stand out. The blowfish are the ones that are always puffing themselves up in order to look bigger and more important than they really are. The whales are the "big" kids on campus, the most popular ones that tend to swim only with their own kind. It's not that they ignore the other fish, it's just that they are so big, they don't even see the smaller fish. The ones that will become your friends, those that are friendly, sociable, and like to play, are the dolphins.

Tell your teenager that it is largely up to him where he decides to swim in the vast fish bowl that is high school.

First Job

Getting that first job is exciting for your child. She no longer
has to ask you for some of the things that she wants. Just as
receiving her driver's license gives her a certain amount of
freedom, so does getting a job. It is freedom "to" and it is freedom "from." It's freedom to . . . go to the movies with friends.
It's freedom to . . . buy that blouse parents think is too expensive. It's freedom from . . . having to ask parents for an
advance on allowance for a special occasion. It's freedom
from . . . being under the financial thumb of parents. This
ritual shows your child those freedoms, along with the
responsibilities, of having her own income.

When your child knows she has the job and what the hourly
pay rate will be, take her out to a nice dinner at one of her
favorite restaurants. Celebrate the fact that she will soon
earn her own income. Keep a copy of the restaurant check or
a copy of the receipt. When you get home, sit down with her
and review the evening. Talk about what you had to eat, then
bring up the cost. Point out how many hours she would have
had to work in order to pay for that meal. Tell her to try to
keep those things in mind when planning what to spend her
paycheck on.

Speaking of planning, now would be a good time to talk
about budgeting. Sit down with paper and pen and plot out
how much she needs to put aside for big purchases, like a
car. Plan out how much gas and insurance will cost for that
car. Stress responsibilities first, then fun, just like at home.
Show her a copy of the household budget and how little a
percentage is given to entertainment. Ask her to think in

terms of percentages instead of numbers. You can also use the ritual "Receiving Allowance" (page 60) to drive home the point. Ask her what she sees herself doing in the future. Tell her to think big and talk about what it would take to get there.

On her first day of work, take a picture of her in her uniform or on her way to work and tell her how proud you are of her. Have this picture enlarged on poster paper. When she gets home from work one day, have this picture awaiting her in her room with the words "Congratulations, Ms. Corporate President," (or Marketing "Whiz," or "Rock Star"). Decorate the poster accordingly, for example, draw in a suit or a guitar. Congratulate her again, tell her how proud you are and encourage her to focus on the ultimate goal.

Welcome her to the fast track.

Learning to Drive

Learning to drive is one of your child's biggest steps to independence. It is the first public evidence of adult responsibility. A driver's license represents not only mobility, but freedom, and it frees both you and your child. When your child can drive himself to activities, you will have more time for yourself. Sure, some of that time will be spent worrying, but with the proper instruction and this ritual, your child driving on his own shouldn't be such a nerve-wracking experience.

During the learning process, whether you or a professional driving teacher is in charge, it is easy for your child to focus on the important factors of driving. Right up until the day after he takes his exam and gets his driver's license, he is still worried enough about passing to pay attention. That focus may or may not last much longer than that day. Celebrate the big day in whatever way seems appropriate, then, before he first takes off on his own, do this ritual.

You are going to give your teenager a performance that you hope will make an impact on him regarding driving and focus. Gather together at least six people, more would be better, and give each one a role to play. The following list is your cast:

The road
Stop sign
Speed limit sign
Cross traffic (one to four people)
Radio
Cell phone
Pedestrian (one to four people)
Stray animal

Be creative and try to think of as many possible distractions that occur while driving—you could include bad weather, flying baseballs, and kids playing in the street. Detours and maps could be represented also.

Make signs for your friends to wear and have your teenager sit in a chair in the middle of the room. Yes, there will probably be much rolling of eyes, but try it anyway. Make it into a game and make it easy at first. When the speed limit sign shows up, the driver must look down momentarily. This would be a good time to send an animal out in front of him. Have the person that is the radio have an actual radio in their hands. Have the child turn it on and adjust the volume occasionally. Have that person sitting in front of the driver. When a song comes on that he wants to change, have him change it or put in a CD. The cell phone needs to ring every once in a while. This is supposed to be fun, at least at first.

Borrow someone's glasses, preferably someone who has a very strong prescription. Put these glasses on the driver and tell him that this is what it would be like to drive while drunk. Have people muffle their voices or talk into their hands. If you have weights, put them on the driver's arms and legs and let him know that his reactions will slow down that much or more when driving. Take the glasses off, but leave the weights on. Say that each weight is one drink, so even if your vision is not impaired, your reaction time still is. Take off the weights.

Next, have everyone move quickly from place to place where the driver cannot see them or focus on them very clearly. This represents speeding or driving recklessly.

The last thing you will want to do is to have everyone sit in front of the teenager and ask him to look at each of them and imagine what it would feel like to have any of those people gone from his life. Explain that all the cars on the road have someone's loved ones in them and to remember that fact when friends encourage reckless behavior. That reckless behavior could result in an accident and possibly deprive someone of a friend or family member.

Use the ritual "New Car" (page 15) to help your teen focus on the protectiveness of being inside a car.

You've given your teen a visual to focus on when he feels peer pressure to do something he knows he shouldn't. Remind him that each little thing is an additional distraction from the road and that the main focus of driving is to get from point A to point B safely.

Arrive alive!

First Formal Dance

It is so exciting to go to a formal. Each generation, of course, has its own idea about what a formal *is* and what a formal is *not*. So does each regional area and even each school. I went to the Arts Magnet High School in Dallas where art, theater, dance, and music students mingled. Needless to say we didn't exactly fit into the mainstream. We were very set on expressing our individuality, so you can probably imagine what our dances looked like. By the time he or she is old enough to attend a formal, your child, too, will want to express individuality. Try to keep this in mind when you are helping your child pick out a formal outfit or decide what kind of flowers to buy. I'm including three rituals here, one for girls, one for boys, and one for the big evening itself. Each will help keep your focus, and theirs, too, on the deeper meanings of the dance and all the activities that go with it.

For the Girls

Okay, Mom, you're up. Your daughter is going to really get into looking for just the right dress, shoes, bag, and so forth. Before your first big shopping day, set the budget for it all. That way, if your daughter finds a dress she loves, but it takes up all of the budget, she will understand that she will have to wear shoes she already has and probably borrow one of your evening bags. Stick to your guns. It's easy to get swept up in the excitement and then regret it once the credit card bill comes. This will also show your daughter that you are serious when it comes to money issues.

When that bit of nasty work is out of the way, you can have some fun! Have your daughter create a list of some of the details she is looking for—hemline length, bodice shape, type of material, and color. Color is one of the most important. The following is a list of colors and their meanings. Show this list to your daughter and ask her to pick out a color that describes how she wants to feel on the big night:

- *Black*—Elegant with a touch of mystery and intrigue
- *White*—Carefree and light
- *Brown*—Down to earth
- *Red*—Vibrant, full of life and energy
- *Orange*—Fun and socially active
- *Yellow*—Joyful, friendly, and personable
- *Green*—Thoughtful and considerate of others
- *Blue*—Intelligent and a lively conversationalist
- *Purple*—Regal and proud (this color is good for potential prom queens)
- *Pastels*—All of the above definitions, only softened

Most girls have some idea of what they are looking for, but if she isn't looking for anything in particular and just wants something to jump out at her, that's okay, too.

Plan a whole day out shopping. Include lunch, and maybe even dinner, while you are out. Put on your most comfortable shoes and hit the malls. This may take more than one trip. Don't make it a general shopping day, either. This is all about your daughter, and she'll love you for it.

Once she has found the dress of her dreams, it's your turn to do a little shopping. In secret. This is a good time to present your daughter with a trinket of some kind. A piece of jewelry to go with her dress would be perfect. As would a handbag or an ornament for her hair, especially if she spent her whole budget on the dress alone. You could also use this occasion to hand down a family heirloom that she has always loved. Keep hold of this item until the day of the formal, however. The ritual at the end will show you how to give it to her.

For the Boys

Okay, Dad, your turn. Although you won't be spending as much time helping your son find a tux, it *is* an important step. Your son may want to match the color of his tie and cummerbund to his date's dress. Dressing for men is always easier than dressing for women. Especially for a formal occasion.

Where your son will need help is in picking out the right flowers for his date. Flowers have a language all their own and although he will want to match or at least complement the color of his date's dress with her corsage, he might also want to know what each flower means. Besides, it will really impress his date when he tells her the meaning of her corsage. Here are some of the most common flowers and their meanings:

- *Apple blossom*—Preference and good fortune
- *Baby's breath*—Everlasting love, happiness, a pure heart
- *Bluebell*—Humility, constancy

- *Camellia*—Admiration, perfection, loveliness
- *Camellia (red)*—You are a flame in my heart
- *Camellia (pink)*—Longing for you
- *Camellia (white)*—Adorable
- *Carnation*—Bonds of affection, health and energy, fascination
- *Carnation (red)*—Admiration
- *Carnation (pink)*—I'll never forget you
- *Carnation (purple)*—whimsical, changeable
- *Carnation (white)*—Sweet and lovely, innocent, pure love
- *Chrysanthemum*—Cheerfulness, you're a wonderful friend
- *Chrysanthemum (red)*—I love you
- *Chrysanthemum (white)*—Truth
- *Dahlia*—Good taste
- *Daisy*—Innocence, loyal love, purity, faith, cheer, simplicity
- *Forget-me-not*—True love, memories, remembrance
- *Gardenia*—You're lovely, secret love, refinement, joy
- *Gladiolus*—Love at first sight, strength of character, generosity
- *Heather (pink)*—Good luck
- *Heather (lavender)*—Admiration
- *Heather (white)*—Wishes will come true, good luck
- *Hibiscus*—Delicate beauty
- *Iris*—Faith, hope, wisdom, valor, eloquence

- *Lavender*—Devotion
- *Lily*—Purity
- *Orchid*—Love, beauty, refinement
- *Rose (red)*—Love, I love you
- *Rose (pink)*—Perfect happiness
- *Rose (white)*—Eternal love, innocence, heavenly
- *Rose (yellow)*—Friendship
- *Rose (red and white)*—Togetherness, unity
- *Rosebud*—Beauty and youth
- *Snapdragon*—Gracious lady
- *Sunflower*—Loyalty, you are splendid
- *Tulip*—Declaration of love
- *Violet*—Faithfulness
- *Zinnia*—Friendship

Now it's your turn to do a little shopping. In secret. This is a good time to present your son with a trinket of some kind. Use this occasion to hand down a family heirloom, like an antique pocket watch he has always admired. Or you could buy him a new wallet or money clip. Keep hold of this item until the day of the formal, however. The ritual at the end will show you how to give it to him.

The Big Night

On prom night, there will be the obligatory rituals including the presentation of the corsage and taking the photos, but before those happen, you can give your son or daughter the special gift you have for them. Present it with a flourish. If it is an heirloom, tell the story behind it. Let your child know that this item is for special occasions *only* and you will keep it safe between those occasions. Tell your child that he or she will take full possession of this gift once he or she moves out of your house. Encourage your child to have a good time on this night and to be safe.

Try not to shed too many tears as you watch your son or daughter drive away on the way to their first formal. Yes, your child is growing up, but you still have a few more years before independence day. Celebrate with your spouse by having a date night yourselves. If you are single, spend the evening going through your own yearbooks with happy remembrances of times past.

Graduating from High School

A lot of pomp and circumstance surrounds the rite of passage that is high school graduation. Many high school graduates will soon be leaving home for college. If college is not in the offing, it won't be long until home is left behind for a place of their own. Gone are the days of mandatory schooling. This ritual shows your graduate the wide world that awaits him.

There is a great deal of chaos both right before and right after graduation: college decisions, finals, the senior prom, obligatory family celebrations, parties with friends, and so forth. Somewhere in the middle of all this, you need to find at least a couple of hours to be alone with your teenager. If possible, both parents should participate in this ritual.

If necessary, kidnap your kid, but don't tell him where you are going. Pack a picnic lunch or dinner. Include foods from places that you know your teenager wants to visit. In with the food, pack a world atlas with his name written on the inside and inscribed with the graduation date.

Now drive to your destination: a parking lot or an empty field close to a major airport where you can watch the planes take off. Present the atlas to your child and tell him that the whole world is now his. Sit on the car's hood and watch the planes take off. Try to guess what exotic destinations they are headed to. Look up these places and read about them—population, altitude, what other cities are close enough to visit.

Bring out the picnic and, as you eat, look up the location where the dish originated. Try to imagine how it must differ from the local version. Talk about what the natives of those other lands must think of *your* local foods. Try to find similarities in spices or main ingredients.

Before heading back home, wish your child good luck in his travels. Tell him to always leave a trail to find his way back home and admonish him to drop you a postcard every once in a while.

The whole world awaits him and there is very little that he can't accomplish in his travels even if he never leaves his hometown.

Fair winds!

The Sex Talk

This is a toughie and should be tackled delicately and in accordance with your own beliefs. It will be embarrassing—probably for both of you. A plethora of tools are available to help you get through this. You can check out wonderful books and even videotapes from your local library. The Internet has some remarkably helpful resources. Even your family physician can give you some ideas on how to proceed. After your talk and subsequent advice, do this ritual to drive home the point that although sexual intercourse is a pleasurable experience, it also carries consequences. It also shows your child that a relationship including sex requires work.

This ritual can be done one of two ways; the first one requires a great deal more work on the parents' part, but it is ultimately the more satisfying.

With your child plan and prepare an entire meal from beginning to end. If possible, both parents should be involved in this process. During the meal preparation, explain that your child's body is like the kitchen, and like a kitchen, she will want to always keep it clean or she could become ill. The foods stored in the kitchen are the advice and ideas of others. Take this opportunity to explain that your child will be getting information from a lot of different sources—some good, some bad. Explain that just like there are rotten foods, there is rotten advice. Let her know that just as *you* have never fed her rotten food, you would also never give her bad advice.

Tell your child also that the work to prepare a great meal is similar to the work that is required of a relationship that involves sex. It takes lots of preparation to have a great relationship and it becomes better when both people are totally devoted to a great meal.

When the meal is ready to be served, set a beautiful table and savor each bite from the appetizer all the way to dessert and everything in between. Let your child know that the meal is like the sexual part of the relationship, all flavor and enjoyment, but now she understands the work behind it that makes it so great.

Involve your child in the cleanup process also and tell her that this phase is the unglamorous side of the relationship. That it's not just work or fun, but that life is messy also and it has to be cleaned up from time to time.

If you don't cook, take your child to a nice restaurant and arrange with the management for a tour behind the scenes. Take her from the preparation area all the way through to the dishwashing area. Stress the same lessons at each phase.

Whichever one you choose, it should bring home the lesson that there is more to sex than the technical or fun part of it. You cook because you love it, yes, but it also takes work.

Sometime within the next week, unexpectedly take your child to a fast-food restaurant, one where you can see the kitchen. Point out that the food isn't nearly as good and takes much less time to prepare and consume. Explain that that is what casual sex is like, not nearly as memorable or enjoyable. The work of a relationship makes it all worthwhile.

New Sibling

When a new sibling arrives in the house there is such joy and pride that all other emotions get swept away in the excitement—at least for a while. The other children in the house may react in a number of ways, from joy to jealousy and everything in between. It is usually children under the age of twelve who have the most difficulty adjusting.

Teenagers tend to have their own interests and will not feel as slighted as younger children if they don't get as much attention. The first part of this ritual is to show those older siblings that not only are they still loved and wanted, but that there is even more love in the house than before. The second part is a little more practical and a way to make sure everybody gets some of your undivided attention and time.

For this ritual, you will need several things: a large jar, large stones (one for each family member, they must all fit loosely inside the jar), color markers, a bag of pebbles, a pitcher of water, and a bag of craft sticks (Popsicle size, fifty or more).

As soon as possible after the baby arrives, sit down with all of your other children. Ask them about things that Mommy and Daddy used to help them with, but they now do by themselves—brushing teeth, bathing, fixing snacks, getting dressed, going potty, eating. List everything you can possibly think of. Next, tell them that all those things must be done for the new baby, because the baby can't do them for himself. That takes time. It takes time away from them, but it doesn't ever take love away from them.

Hand each child a stone to decorate, representing himself or herself. At the same time decorate one for each parent and one for the new baby. Decorate the jar with the family name. Place all the stones *except the baby's stone* in the jar and tell your children that this is the family. Shake up the jar and tell them that the stones shift from time to time, touching each other in different ways. This means that you spend different amounts of time with different family members.

Present the bag of pebbles and explain that the pebbles represent all the things that have to be done during the day, including the things you have already talked about. But Mommy and Daddy have more pebbles that anyone else, because they have more to do, including taking care of the baby. Pour the pebbles into the jar. Leave quite a bit of open space in the jar. Explain that you may be asking everyone to help out more because there is now more to do. Shake the jar and let the pebbles settle into place.

Pick up the pitcher of water and slowly pour it into the jar. As you do so, explain that the water is the love that the family has for one another. When the jar is full, put the cap on and rotate the jar, showing each child how the love helps make everything move around easier. Tell them that there will always be love.

Take the cap off the jar and point out the level of the water. Now add the stone that represents the baby and comment on how the water level rose. Adding the baby just increased the love in the household for *everybody*. Place the jar where everyone in the household can view it on a daily basis.

The next part of this ritual involves the craft sticks. Explain to your kids that you understand that they need your time and attention also and it will be difficult to remember that sometimes. These sticks will be a reminder of time, but it will be up to each child to judge how much he or she will need. Mark the sticks with different amounts of time: five minutes, fifteen minutes, half an hour, an hour. Make several of each. Put these sticks in a bowl that is accessible to everyone. Tell each child that when they need Mommy or Daddy's *undivided* attention for something, let's say a homework assignment, he or she is to try to judge how much time will be necessary and present the appropriate stick to the parent.

It's up to you how strict you wish to be with this time limit. Make sure the children also understand that there are a limited number of times the large chunks of time can be used.

Make it a point to set a time limit for yourself to give each child the time needed. For example, let the children know that when they present you with a time stick, you will make that time for them sometime within the next hour, because you may not be able to drop what you are doing right that minute. This ritual helps you as a parent to recognize that each child does need some time alone with you. It is easy to forget, sometimes, in the hustle and bustle of daily living, especially with a new baby. It helps the kids to better use their time.

Congratulations on your new arrival! May your house be filled to overflowing with love and happiness.

Older Sibling Leaving Home

When one of your children leaves home to go to college or to get his own place, he can leave an awful hole for the children left behind. Even with sibling rivalry and the petty bickering that sometimes goes on, younger children look up to and admire their older siblings. When your children are close in age, it is easier, but when a teenager leaves behind a six- or ten-year-old, the transition is never easy. This short and simple ritual is meant more for that kind of age difference and is designed for younger children. Older children typically do not require reassurance that their big brother or sister still loves them and won't be gone forever.

* * *

This ritual is in two parts. The first part is for the siblings to do together. Encourage your older child to do this to help ease the transition. Have the one moving out give something to the younger child. It needs to be something of sentimental value to the older child—a trophy, a favorite poster, a cherished book. At the same time, have the older child tell the younger one, "Take care of this for me and whenever you feel sad, just remember that I will be back every once in a while. And when I come back I expect this _____ to be in as good condition as it is now." This lets the child know that the older sibling isn't leaving for good, especially since he left behind a cherished possession.

After your older child has moved out, take some time to explain to the younger one why it hurts. Tell him that he is connected to everyone he loves by an invisible string in his heart. When a beloved person isn't there with him, that string pulls and tugs at his heart and that's why he misses that person. Assure him that the older sibling feels that tugging, too, and when that tugging gets really strong, like during holidays and special occasions, the older sibling will let that tug carry him home for a visit. In the meantime, tell your child that he needs to focus on someone or something else in his heart that is closer to him. A favorite activity, toy, or person. This won't take the place of his older sibling, but he won't feel the tugging quite so much.

When the first visit happens (probably during a holiday), make sure your older child asks about the item he left behind. Have him praise the younger one for taking such good care of it. Give them some time alone together to get an ice cream cone, go to the park, or just talk. As much as you miss your older child, your younger child does too.

Enjoy the time you have together and cherish the thought that your children truly love one another.

First Period

A girl's first menstrual period is a very special time. She will begin to truly see herself as a woman instead of as a little girl, although she is not quite there yet. As she nears the world of women, she is unsure of herself and her place in that vast sisterhood. This is an exciting, yet uncertain, time. This ritual will help your daughter to see that things are changing and it will also help parents to better understand that their daughter is growing up.

When you see your daughter begin to show the signs of starting her period encourage her to think of it in a positive way. Discourage the idea that her period is a "curse." Avoid negative terminology such as "the curse," or "on the rag." Tell her that starting her period is not only indicative of being able to have children, but that it is also a symbol for her creativity. Because of this, she is now able to come to a deeper understanding of how to create all kinds of new things, not just children.

Make the day she starts her period into a celebration. Take off work and take her out of school, if you can. If that is not feasible then explain to her that the very next non-work/non-school day will be *her* day to celebrate.

Start by having Dad send her flowers or buy her a special gift to congratulate her on becoming a young woman. A small piece of jewelry is very appropriate. She will probably be a bit embarrassed at Dad's "knowing," but she will feel special—and that is the point.

Make the day a mom-and-daughter thing. If your girl-friends, older sisters, or other older female family members are open to it, plan a lunch at your daughter's favorite restaurant with the "sisterhood." Have each woman explain her personal remedies for the discomforts that can occur during this time. Explain the symptoms to look for that will tell her when to expect her period. Show her how to chart it so she will be prepared.

After lunch, take your daughter shopping for something specific. This would be a good time to begin allowing some more grown-up things like makeup or pierced ears if you haven't already. Your daughter will be excited at being allowed something more adult to wear or have for her room.

That night, have a special family dinner. Make it a celebration along the lines of a birthday party with congratulatory cards or even a cake.

Your daughter has just entered a whole new world. Congratulations!

Moving with Kids

Uprooting a family and moving them used to be much more traumatic than it is today. Ours is a transient society and we seldom live our entire lives in the same house or neighborhood. We move to other cities for better jobs, climate, or schools. Whatever the reason, this ritual will help ease that transition for you and your family.

Take a morning or an afternoon to sit down with your kids to tell them about all the new and wonderful things they will find in their new place. Have brochures from the chamber of commerce to show them. Having done a little bit of research ahead of time, tell them about places of specific interest to each. Does your teenage son love to surf? Are you moving away from the beach? Tell him about the snowboarding activities in your new place. Let him know that you understand it's not exactly the same, but it's close and he just might find that he likes snowboarding better than surfing. Does your ten-year-old girl love to play soccer? Research the school team or local leagues for her ahead of time. Whatever your children's interests, from music and theater to gymnastics, research that extracurricular activity and find out what is available for them. This will show them that you really do have their best interests at heart even if they did not have a say in the decision to move.

Younger children have an easier time adjusting to new circumstances and places, but they will still need reassurance from you that everything will be okay. Their biggest fears will typically be associated with making new friends and "fitting in" in their new environment. Take some time to sit down with them and literally "make friends." Get a book of paper dolls and make up names, faces, and personalities for possible new friends. Dress these new friends appropriately and pack them in the child's suitcase that she will have with her during the move. That way, she won't feel quite as alone. With these new friends pack photos of the friends they will be leaving behind so she will have her memories as company during the trip.

For older children and teenagers, take them to a favorite place. This could be a fishing hole, beach, coffee shop, or even a mall. Remind them of the first time they set foot in this place and how unfamiliar it was. Bring to mind the adventure in discovering the place and in finding out what it had to offer. Let them know that the new places will be just as good, maybe even better. And there will be adventure in discovering the places unique to your destination. Assure them also, with a sense of humor, that some of their old favorites will probably be around in the new place, too, and when they get homesick they can always go to McDonald's and have fries and they will taste *exactly* the same.

Have a number of keys made for your new place and give one to each child. When you arrive, make a game out of having each child unlock the door to the new family home. Whatever you do, stay excited about the move, and that attitude will transfer to your children.

May your moving day be sunny, warm, and, most of all, stress-free!

Divorce

Divorce is one of the hardest things to go through, for both adults and children. This ritual will help your child understand that even though Mom and Dad are no longer together, the child is not to blame. It also shows the child that the connection between parent and child will remain no matter what else changes. This ritual is similar to the one on divorce in Chapter 3, "Friends and Family" (page 43), but with variations to include children. Divorce is final and, as parents, you will have a piece of paper to prove it, but your child won't have that certification. He will need something just as concrete. This ritual provides that, symbolizing the separation between Mom and Dad, but leaving in place the link between each parent and each child.

You will need several thick pieces of biodegradable rope (something large enough to write on)—two pieces for each child, and one for Mom and Dad. You will also need a sharp knife or scissors, a pot of earth, and a marker.

Gather the whole family together either before or after the actual court date. Take one of the ropes and write Mom's name on one end and Dad's on the other. Write each child's name on two ropes. Tie one rope to Mom's end and tie the other one to Dad's. Have your children hold on to their ends of the two ropes. Take turns thanking one another for all the joyful times that you have all had as a family. Relive the good memories only. It is important for the children to remember that even though Mom and Dad are going their separate ways that they did have fun together. Then tell your children that those fun times will continue, separately, with each parent.

Take this time, also, to stress to your children that the reasons that Mom and Dad are breaking up have nothing to do with them. Tell them often, because children, especially young children, tend to think that if they had behaved better more often or done something better, Mom and Dad wouldn't be getting divorced.

The next thing you will want to do is cut the cord between Mom and Dad. Take turns doing this to represent joint responsibility. Say the following while you cut the cord.

> *I release you with love and hope for you only*
> *the best in life.*

After you have cut the cord turn to your children one at a time and say:

> *The tie between* us *can never be cut, for I am*
> *your father/mother and always will be.*

Place the scissors or knife, point down, in the pot of soil to symbolize an end to conflict.

If there is only one child, then that child can keep those cords in their room or hang them up in a special place on the wall. If there is more than one child, hang the strand in a central room of the house. To make it even more permanent, you can frame the strand. Keep the cords in the home of the parent who has primary custody. If parents have joint custody, then keep the strand for Mom at Dad's house and vice-versa. That way the child is always reminded of the parent who is absent.

Note: If one parent, for whatever reason, does not want to participate in this ritual, it can still be done. Simply use a photo to represent the missing parent.

Remarriage

Another toughie for kids is the remarriage of a parent. Blending families takes a great deal of patience and understanding. The most important thing in any remarriage is to make *all* the kids feel like they belong to the *same family*. The best way to do this is to include all the children in the wedding ceremony in one capacity or another. If that is not possible, do this ritual sometime soon after the wedding. It's a long and rocky road, but perhaps this ritual will provide you with a set of shock absorbers right from the beginning.

This ritual continues the theme of the previous one—divorce. Except this time all you will need is one long rope or thick ribbon and a marker. Write the parent and step-parent's name, respectively, on each end of the rope, then have each child write his or her name somewhere on the rope. After all the kids have done this, tie a knot over each child's name and explain that all of them are each knotted into both their biological parent and their step-parent's lives.

After this is done say:

> *All those here are one family*
> *May our lives combine as easily as this knot is tied*
> *And may our togetherness make us strong and happy*

Display the rope someplace prominent, and never forget that you are all tied together.

Empty Nest

Ah, the joys of having the house all to yourself. Ah, the heartbreak of having the house all to yourself. When your last child leaves home for good, your feelings are obviously mixed. I'm not talking about going off to college when it is understood that the child will be coming home weekends and holidays. I'm talking about when your child packs up all her stuff and moves to her first apartment or rents her first house. She will be leaving some stuff behind and her room will still be decorated the same way. This three-part ritual is for the parents to perform after the child has left, to help ease that transition.

You will want to evaluate the child's room and think about how you would like to change it. The amount of time that passes between your child's leaving and when this final transformation takes place is entirely up to you. It could be a matter of days or it could take as long as a year. Don't make it so long, however, that the room becomes a shrine. During this process, enter the room occasionally and take a look around. Go ahead and relive the memories that arise.

If you see a blue ribbon from a swim meet, take the time to think about the preparation that swim meet required. The long hours practicing. The joy on your child's face when she won. The pride in your heart when you watched her win. After reliving that good time, take the item that invoked the memory and put it in a box. Each time you enter the room do this same small ritual. Find an item that brings up memories, relive the memories, then pack away the item. As I said earlier, this can take place over a weekend or over a year.

Once the packing is under way and the room is approximately half empty, you will proceed to phase two of this ritual. By the time you reach this point, you will be pretty sure what you will want to use the room for. Perhaps you want to turn it into a guest room or a space for making crafts or sewing. Maybe it will become a library or a den. It could be a combination of any of the above—or something completely different.

Now is the time to start changing the room to its new incarnation. Start moving furniture, paint the walls, take measurements, replace the window treatments, pull up the carpeting. With each trip into the room, you will not only be reliving memories and packing those memories away, you will also be bringing in something new, even if it is only an idea or a tape measure at first. You will find the process beginning to speed up, and before you know it, your child's room will be transformed into something completely new and different and you will have relived some of the best memories from her "growing up" years. Store her stuff in the attic or the basement for the day when she will want to retrieve it or for your own future walks down memory lane.

Now, on to phase three: You may find that you have a lot more free time on your hands once your child has moved. This can contribute to the empty feeling in the house, because it is not only empty of the *presence* of your child but it is also bereft of her *activities*. Think back to the time before you had children. What did you do for fun? Make an effort to do those things again. Spend more time with friends. Go to the movies more often. Enroll in a class that you have always wanted to take. Buy season tickets to the theater or symphony. Make plans. Make plans that *don't involve children*, whether your own or other people's. It's time to be a little selfish and do what *you* want to do instead of what other people *think* you should be doing. Life isn't over because your children have all moved away. Quite the contrary, the volume just got turned up.

Tune the radio station to the music you like and dance your way through the rest of your life.

5

Nature's Wheel

SEASONAL CHANGES

WHEN HUMANKIND was an agriculture-based society, rituals were held to celebrate the turning of the seasons. Planting and harvesting were only two among many celebrations throughout the year. Today, we go from our climate-controlled houses to our climate-controlled cars to our climate-controlled workplaces and back again without ever touching foot to grass. Because we spend so much of our time indoors, we've lost touch with nature and rarely notice the seasons are changing until the change is well under way.

This chapter is dedicated to rituals concerning the changing of the seasons. Some changes are traditional indications like the first snowfall of Winter, while others are not so traditional, such as turning on the air conditioning for the first time in the Summer. (Here in southeast Texas that can be as early as March!)

By first noticing and then celebrating the changing seasons, we better attune ourselves with the natural rhythms of Mother Earth and find ourselves more respectful of Her constantly changing wardrobe.

The Green of Spring

Spring is such a hopeful time. We begin to see a hint of what the world will look like come Summer. Color is returning to a world that has been bereft of warmth. It doesn't take long after we notice that first bud that the trees burst into leaf, flowers into bloom, and the crackle of cold brown grass turns to the whisper of a soft green carpet. Do this ritual when you notice the first green of Spring. This green can be anything from a flowering bud to a blade of grass to an unfurling leaf.

Take your place in front of the first green and address it:

> *I welcome you—first indication of warm weather*
>   *to follow.*
> *I welcome you—budding new life.*
> *I welcome you—fresh green sunshine.*
> *Even though Winter is not yet over, you bring hope*
>   *that color and warmth will once again return*
>   *and that the wheel of the year is turning.*
> *I honor the miracle of returning growth as I bring*
>   *your cousins into my home.*

Take time on this day to bring fresh flowers or a new plant into your home. Wherever you place it say the following words as you do so:

> *May the freshness of this plant (these flowers)*
> *encourage the freshness of Springtime to enter*
> *my home.*

Open a window. If the temperature is bearable, leave the window open all day. If it's still chilly outside, then leave it open only temporarily. As the breeze enters the window say:

> *Fresh breezes of Spring, blow through my home*
> *and carry away the staleness of Winter.*
> *Bring newness, growth, color, and vibrancy into*
> *my home.*

This ritual can be done in your office, workshop, or any place where you spend a great deal of time. Remember to throw out the flowers as they begin to wilt and cut dead leaves off the plant. You want to keep things as fresh as possible during Spring.

The second part of this ritual can be repeated on the first truly warm day of Spring when you *want* to keep all the windows open all day.

Spring is an excellent time to think about what we would like to begin in our lives. New Year's resolutions are better to make and easier to keep when made in the Spring. We get a little push from Mother Nature as we are inspired by the growth all around us.

Here's to Spring and new beginnings!

Spring Cleaning

Sometime soon after we've welcomed Spring into our homes, we feel the need to sweep away the dreariness of Winter. It's Spring-cleaning time. The house is stale from being closed up for months, and we need freshness. The ritual here is a very simple one, but you can add extra power to it by repeating the second part of the ritual "The Green of Spring" from the previous pages before you begin this one.

Gather all the tools of Spring cleaning: mops, buckets, detergents, even family members! Before beginning, say:

> *With every speck of dust and piece of dirt we*
> *wipe away, we wipe away the old and unneeded*
> *from our lives. We leave behind freshness and*
> *clear the space for newness to enter our lives.*

Don't forget to clean out the fireplace, but don't throw away those ashes! Plants love wood ash, so sprinkle the ashes from your fireplace out in the flowerbeds of the garden or even in your houseplants.

Scour away!

Swim into Summer

For those of us who live in the South, Summer begins long before the calendar says it does. When I was a kid, Summer started long before school was out, so in Dallas, Texas, that occasion was not an effective marker. Neither was Memorial Day. And by the third week in June (the official "first day of Summer") I had been wearing shorts for at least a couple of months—maybe longer. I always knew it was Summer when the pools started opening on the weekends or when we went to the lake to go water skiing for the first time during the season. So to me, at least, Summer revolves around the water. This ritual celebrates summer with the first swim of the season.

* * *

Hitting the water for the first time in the Summer can, quite literally, take your breath away. The greens and blues of the water in which you frolic are not only refreshing for the body, but for the soul as well. Water is both calming and rejuvenating. Whether you splash into the ocean, lake, river, or the pool down the block, drink a large glass of refreshing, ice-cold water first and say:

This water nourishes my body.

Jump in. If you don't swim, then gently lower yourself into the water. (If you don't like water at all, at least make a symbolic gesture by dipping just your toe.) After you surface say:

This water nourishes my spirit.
Hail and welcome Summertime!

Enjoy your summer swims!

Fall Color

When the leaves first begin to change color in the Fall it is hardly noticeable. But suddenly one day you leave the house and a riot of color greets you from the trees. The grass is fading to a dull brown and the earth changes from the bright greens of summer to the warm reds, yellows, and oranges of Autumn. It's quite a contrast that as the days turn colder, the colors become warmer. Celebrate nature's beautiful change with this ritual.

Pack a picnic basket with foods that mimic the colors of the fall leaves; amazingly enough, they are the foods that are traditionally associated with the waning of the year—apples, nuts, pumpkins, squash. Think of the cornucopia of Thanksgiving and you're on the right track. As a matter of fact, this picnic could be a feast similar to that offered at Thanksgiving, just a little earlier in the year. Fall is the perfect time to reflect on the Summer just past and all the activities you have completed.

Scout out a spot where you are surrounded by brilliant trees. Since this is the evening of the year, have your picnic just before sunset. During your picnic, be thankful for the abundance in your life. Since this is the season of harvest, try to focus on what you are harvesting in your life. As the sky turns as brilliant as the trees with the setting of the sun, enjoy your meal. When you are finished, show appreciation of the harvest by leaving small pieces of your picnic behind for those animals that are storing food for the winter. Breathe in the colors and bid them to keep you warm during the approaching Winter.

Winter White

Depending on where you live, there are many varying signs to indicate the beginning of Winter. To those in northern climes, typically the first snowfall is the harbinger of Winter. For those in the warmer states, it's usually the first frost. Folks on the Gulf Coast can go years or even decades without seeing a single flake of snow. So this ritual of Winter is a celebration of Winter white, whether it's a light frosting on the grass or several inches of new snow in the yard.

First Frost

After the leaves have started turning the brilliant reds and golds of Fall, there comes that day. You know the one I'm talking about. It's the day we walk outside, step off the pavement, and the grass crunches beneath our feet. There is a shimmer in the air and the rooftops sparkle with a clean, crisp hint of winter to come. The cold air stings our lungs and our breath escapes in steam. Before returning indoors to grab that extra layer of clothing, do this short ritual.

Bend down, touch a bare hand to the frost and say:

> *May Winter's touch bring peace and rest to*
> *   the earth,*
> *And pass as easily as my hand slides over the ice.*

Celebrate this early sign of winter by reinforcing it. Eat something that resembles the frost, like a snow cone or ice cream cone. A frosted cookie or piece of coconut cream pie would work well, too! Welcome to Winter!

First Snowfall

Awakening to a world covered with a white blanket of freshness invokes childhood memories of sledding, building snowmen, or otherwise playing in the snow. Many adults ignore the fun and beauty of snow and see only the necessities and the hassles. Shoveling the walk and putting chains on the car become primary concerns. Once the wintertime responsibilities of adulthood have been taken care of, turn any of the following into a ritual of welcoming Winter. Remind yourself of the joys of snow.

Be a child and play!

- Build a snowman.
- Make snow ice cream.
- Build a snow fort and pelt passersby with snowballs.
- Have a snowball fight with your kids.
- Make snow angels.
- Go sledding (even if your "sled" is just a piece of cardboard).
- Try to catch snowflakes on your tongue.

The joys of snow are not just for children. After playing, you will come home with your cheeks red and your nose running. The smile on your face and the purity of childhood pleasures, however, will awaken the joys of Winter in your heart and soul.

Thermostat Switch

Changing the thermostat from heat to air conditioning and from air conditioning back to heat signals not only a change in seasons, but a change in the atmosphere of the house. We are mentally preparing ourselves for Summer or Winter. These rituals will get you into the swing of things.

Summer Switch

Usually, at least in our house, the air conditioning doesn't get turned on until we are sitting around with the windows open, fans running, and find that we are *still* sweating. The air conditioner may get turned on in March for a week and then the heat goes on again the next week. This is Texas after all, and as the saying goes. "If you don't like the weather, stick around ten minutes, it'll change." But even though it may get cold again briefly, we know that Summer is not far away. So, before switching on the air conditioning, pour yourself a favorite Summer beverage. This could be a glass of iced tea, lemonade, or even a beer. Whatever you choose, make sure it is ice cold. Notice how the glass sweats and remind yourself that you don't have to do that. You have air conditioning. Ah, the joys of modern living! Take the beverage outside and pour a little bit of it on the unit itself and say:

> *May the cold air of this unit remain as cold as*
> *this beverage throughout the summer.*

Go back in the house, close all the windows and turn off all the fans, then make your way to the thermostat. Before you turn it on, be aware of the heat and stuffiness of the room. After you turn on the air conditioner, make your way to the closest vent. Hold your beverage in one hand and place the other hand in front of the vent. Remain there until the cold air matches the temperature of your drink. Have a fun Summer!

Winter Switch

Begin with an unlit candle, preferably a red one, for red represents Fire and warmth. If you have to light a furnace before turning on your heat for the first time, take the candle and the matches/lighter with you. Stand in front of the furnace and light the candle. As you do so, say:

> *May the flame of this candle grow and may its*
> *heat spread throughout the house and keep us*
> *warm during the coming winter.*

Light the match with the candle, *not* the other way around. You are symbolically transferring the heat of the candle to the match that will light the furnace and heat your home. Light the furnace with that match. Take the lighted candle with you to the thermostat and repeat the above phrase as you turn on the heat. Proceed to the closest vent; hold the candle in one hand and place the other one in front of the vent. Once the air warms and begins circulating throughout the house, you can extinguish the candle.

You can also use this ritual when lighting your fireplace for the first time during the season.

Ah, climate control . . . it's a wonderful thing.

Seasonal Changes in Closets

Putting on that first sundress in the Summer or that first plush sweater in the Winter is truly a sign that the seasons have changed. During the transition, we may pull one or two items out of storage and our closets become a mixture of seasons. Eventually, though, the time comes when you know you won't be wearing those shorts or that coat and scarf again until next year. On the day that the clothes exchange happens, try these rituals to make the transition less tedious.

Winter to Summer

Summer clothes feel so good after a Winter of being covered up. Lightweight, flowing fabrics reveal bare arms and legs and make us feel more free. Summer clothes lift the heaviness of Winter not only from our closets and dressers, but from our lives as well. If nothing else, Summer clothes sure take up a lot less room.

First you must remove Winter from your closet. As you are packing away the woolens and tweeds, imagine Winter being packed with them. Inspect each item carefully for any needed repairs. Have your sewing kit handy so you can make those repairs on the spot. If the repairs are beyond your ability, send your clothes out to be repaired before you pack them away. You will appreciate this when the clothes come out of storage next Winter ready to wear. Also, take the time to think about the last time you wore each item. If it's been more than two years chances are good that you won't ever wear it again. This is the best time to give away those items that no longer appeal to you or that you have simply outgrown.

A few items usually remain in your closets and drawers year-round. You will want to remove these as well, at least temporarily, so you can be more thorough in your cleaning. Dust the shelves and vacuum or sweep the floor of your closet before unpacking your Summer clothes so they have a fresh place to hang.

Before you wake your Summer clothes from their hibernation, visualize them being bound up in knots. As you open those bags, trunks, or drawers that house your clothes, untie those knots by saying:

> *The freedom of Summer is here.*
> *Here in flowing cottons and silks.*
> *May they keep me cool and carefree.*

Choose your favorite casual Summer outfit and wear it as you finish hanging your clothes.

Summer to Winter

Pulling on that cashmere sweater for the first time is almost like pulling security on over your head. The plush feel of wool, corduroy, and leather reminds us of being tucked securely in our beds during raging Winter storms. Being totally enclosed and warm is true contentment, and you know that you are protected from the worst that Mother Nature can throw at you.

First you must remove Summer from your closet. As you are packing away the cottons and silks, imagine Summer being packed with them. Inspect each item carefully for any needed repairs. Have your sewing kit handy so you can make those repairs on the spot. If the repairs are beyond your ability, send your clothes out to be repaired before you pack them away. You will appreciate this when the clothes come out of storage next Summer ready to wear. Also, take the time to think about the last time you wore each item. If it's been more than two years chances are good that you won't ever wear it again. This is the best time to give away those items that no longer appeal to you or that you have simply outgrown.

A few items usually remain in your closets and drawers year-round. You will want to remove these as well, at least temporarily, so you can be more thorough in your cleaning. Dust the shelves and vacuum or sweep the floor of your closet before unpacking your Winter clothes so they have a fresh place to hang.

As you open those bags, trunks, or drawers that house your Winter clothes, visualize a cozy warm cabin with a fire blazing. Pack that cabin into your closet with your Winter clothes by saying:

> *The restfulness of Winter is here.*
> *Here in comforting wool and heavy fabrics.*
> *May they keep me warm and secure.*

Choose your favorite casual Winter outfit and wear it as you finish hanging your clothes.

Enjoy and revel in the feel of your seasonal clothing.

Seasonal Changes in House

Household decorations are no longer just for religious or cultural holidays. Different pillows on the sofa, a change in mantel decorations, or a new tablecloth are all ways to celebrate the seasons. The specific calendar date didn't matter in the previous seasonal rituals. Instead a weather change determined when to celebrate each season. The following rituals are designed to mark the season on the official calendar date.

When the seasons change, decorate your house like you would adorn your body for special occasions. If these dates happen to coincide with a religious holiday for you, all the better for this adds another element to the celebration. Although the dates vary slightly every year, it's never by more than a day or so.

The First Day of Spring

Spring Equinox. Around March 22 is the time when day and night are the same length—equinox. Our modern calendar marks this day as the official first day of Spring. To celebrate the warming of the year and the lengthening of the days, place candles in light colored candlesticks on the mantel. Change the tablecloth and throw pillows to lighter colors; pastels are always good for Spring. Since it is the season for planting and growth, eggs are appropriate decorations as well as baby animals like bunnies and chicks. (*Note:* These may seem like Christian Easter decorations, but they are not intended to be religious decorations, rather as representations of the season of growth. By all means, if your religion uses these symbols and you wish to do so, feel free to assign them religious importance.) After you have placed the decorations around the house, say the following:

> *I welcome the first day of Spring.*
> *May it be a time of growth, not only for the earth,*
> *but for myself and my loved ones as well.*

The First Day of Summer

Summer Solstice. Around June 21 is the time of the longest day of the year. Sunlight graces us with its presence well into the evening. Our modern calendar marks this day as the official first day of Summer. To celebrate the heat of the Summer, replace the pastels of Spring with the vibrant colors of Summer. Change the tablecloth and throw pillows to the jewel tone reds, yellows, blues, and especially the vibrant greens of Summer—candles, too! Because this is the season when plants are in their full growth and vibrancy, place sunflowers on the mantel as a reminder of the Summer sun. A wreath on the door covered in bright summer flowers welcomes guests to your home. After you have placed the decorations around the house, say the following:

> *I welcome the first day of Summer.*
> *May the fullness of this season fill our lives with all*
> *the joys of a garden in full bloom.*

The First Day of Fall

Autumnal Equinox. Around September 22 is the time when day and night are the same length—equinox. Our modern calendar marks this day as the official first day of Fall. To celebrate the cooling of the year and the shortening of the days, place Fall leaves on the mantel or on the wreath on the door. The browns, oranges, and reds of the season are muted and match the colors of the leaves. This is a time of harvest—apples, pumpkins, and nuts are taken in. These items make great decorations for your home—even though, in this country, Thanksgiving is still two months away. After you have placed the decorations around the house, say the following:

> *I welcome the first day of Fall.*
> *May the abundance of this season help us to*
> *   harvest those things in our lives that were*
> *   planted long ago.*

The First Day of Winter

Winter Solstice. Around December 21 is the time of the longest night of the year. Shadows lengthen and darkness intrudes during our days. Our modern calendar marks this day as the official first day of Winter. One way to celebrate the depths of Winter is to remind ourselves that Spring will return. We bring greenery into our homes. Evergreen boughs adorn mantels and doors. Candles in the vibrant colors of summer—red and green—grace tabletops and mantels. Lights hang from the eaves of our homes to bring some light to the long Winter nights. Another way to celebrate is by reveling in the colors of Winter, white-and-blue tablecloths and paper snowflakes hanging from the ceiling as if they are floating down from clouds pregnant with winter. (*Note:* Some of these may seem like Christmas or Hanukkah decorations, but they are not intended to be religious decorations, rather as representations of the season. By all means, if your religion uses these symbols and you wish to do so, feel free to assign them religious importance.) After you have placed the decorations around the house, say the following:

I welcome the first day of Winter.
May the dark and cold of this season bring us
restful dreams and peaceful lives.

Whatever way you decide to decorate your house for the seasons, let the act of decorating be just as important as the finished project. Bring representations of the outside in and be comfortable in each season.

6

Hi-Ho, Hi-Ho,
It's Off to Work We Go

WORK. Is it really a four-letter word? If so, perhaps what makes the job unpleasant is routine. So many people get bored with doing the same thing all the time. On the other hand, people with high-stress jobs often wish for a little workplace boredom now and then.

Whether your particular job is the four-letter variety or not, you'll spend at least a third of your life working. As a culture, we have almost *no* work-related rituals. The ones that do exist tend to be about transitional happenings such as a new job, retirement, or a promotion. Even those few are typically celebrated in only a token way, like the boss taking you to lunch on the company. You might get a cake or a farewell toast, but that's usually the extent of our workplace rituals.

What about all those little happenings in our workday? This section is full of workday rituals that celebrate the everyday things that happen in the place where many of us spend most of our time. There are three different sections in this chapter: "The Ups," "The Downs," and "The Executive Washroom." Let's give that third of our lives extra meaning with rituals that are about more than just bringing home a paycheck.

The Ups

There are lots of peaks you reach during the life of your career. These highs may not be as important emotionally as the highs in your personal life (marriage, family, friends) and their importance is often overlooked. So let's consider them. Why should your working life be undeserving of rituals? This section is devoted to the fun and satisfying times at work. The highs that make your job something to look forward to each day.

New Job

Starting a new job can be nerve-racking. There are new people to meet and work with, new duties to perform, and high expectations from everyone involved. There are always moments of doubt the first day of a new job, and it takes a while to get into the swing of things. Give yourself that time and remember that your new coworkers are nervous as well. With this ritual, you set the intent for a productive and pleasant work experience.

On the first day of your new job, it is typical to meet first with the person who hired you. That person could be anyone from a human resources recruiter to your new boss or your boss's boss. No matter who you meet first, greet that person with your most dazzling smile and an open hand. The ritual of the handshake is an ancient custom. It began as a way for strangers or rivals to show each other that neither was carrying a weapon. It was a show of trust prior to an opening conversation or truce talks. Today presenting an open hand still symbolically shows that you have nothing to hide. A handshake is also an acceptable and a social form of touch (a hug is okay for a friend, but not for a new coworker), and touch is always important when meeting someone new.

What you say to this first person will set your intent. The words will no doubt be words that are spoken many times. The difference is in you and how you feel every time you speak them. Make them into a ritual. Really *think* about what you are saying and mean it! Don't just go on automatic.

While talking with new people imagine a blue light between you and the person to whom you are speaking. This establishes and strengthens communication between the two of you. The words you use will determine how your work life will start.

I'm so pleased to be here.
I am really looking forward to working with you.
Thank you for this opportunity.
I know we will make a great team.

The next step is to meet your new coworkers. As you shake each person's hand try to convey the same attitude and use the blue light with him or her as well. You will find yourself saying the requisite words:

It's nice to meet you.
I'm looking forward to working with you.

While they will respond with things like:

Welcome aboard.
Glad to have you here.

Mean what you say and make eye contact while speaking. Your sincerity will definitely make a good first impression and you will find your new coworkers responding in kind. As the day wears on, you will no doubt grow tired of these words. Don't get lax, though; the last person you meet could be the one you will be working most closely with. Keep it sincere, and you will find yourself settling in to your new job with much less nervousness.

Welcome aboard!

First Big Project

Well, it finally happened. The boss entrusted you with your first big project. Even though that's exciting, it can also be overwhelming. Pulling all the pieces of a project together can seem like a monumental task once you actually start thinking about it. The trick is not to think about the whole as much as you do about each piece. An expression that helps me when I get overwhelmed by a large project is "Inch by inch, life's a cinch. Yard by yard, life is hard." The simple ritual that follows will help you focus on all the details and get past the inertia that sometimes accompanies the beginning of big projects.

Put together a jigsaw puzzle.

Sounds too simple, I know, but it really works. Seeing how each piece fits in with the others helps you concentrate and see all the particulars of any situation. If possible, have a puzzle in your office so when you get stuck on a specific problem, you can take a few moments to clear your mind by focusing on something else. Some people switch over to a computer game like solitaire or something similar. That's okay, but it's more of a distraction than a tool to help you focus. A jigsaw puzzle can be the right tool.

If there is not a space large enough in your work area, consider getting permission to set up an ongoing puzzle in the break room. I once worked for a company that did this, and the boss swore that it increased productivity. If neither possibility will work, you can probably find a jigsaw puzzle software program or an Internet game. (If not, someone needs to invent one.) Ideally though, having actual pieces in your hand is preferable to moving them around on a computer screen.

If it is not possible to set up a puzzle at the job site, keep one going at home and work on it for a few minutes when you arrive after work. You may find yourself resolving issues the next day. Keep a pad and pen next to the puzzle to write down the spur-of-the-moment ideas that will likely occur to you while doing this ritual. Have fun with your first big project. It is such a joy to fit the final piece and see the big picture.

New Boss

Just like getting a new job, getting a new boss can be nerve-racking. What most workers never consider is that the new boss is probably just as nervous as the employees. Do the rituals suggested in "New Job" (page 120) during the initial introductions then follow up with something very simple. Listen. A new boss is always going to have new ideas and different ways of running things. This will upset the status quo, which will upset the workers. People don't like change, and a new boss will most definitely be making changes. Take a deep breath and use the following ritual when you find yourself upset or apprehensive about your new boss.

As you sit at your desk, close your eyes momentarily and imagine a body of water. It could be a swimming pool, river, lake or beach. Even picturing ourselves in a hot tub or bathtub can be soothing. Water represents our emotional side. Get right in and swim around a little. The important aspect of this visualization is that the water be calm and warm. Explore how you really feel about any given situation instead of simply reacting to it. It's too easy to get caught up in the emotional upset of someone else, instead of taking the time to think about the problem first. Try to see it from your new boss's point of view.

As we swim in our minds, we find emotional tranquility. Conjure this image before the first meeting with the new boss and you will find yourself calmly listening to his or her expectations and ideas. Summon this visualization whenever you find yourself upset over something the new boss is doing.

Don't worry, you are not going to drown, but it is a good idea at times like these to try to float and just "go with the flow." Raft up with your coworkers and you'll soon find the boss cheerfully guiding your course downstream.

Promotion

Congratulations! You've been promoted! At work, there's nothing to compare to the joy of being rewarded for a job well done. And a promotion is the ultimate reward! It means that you have earned trust and respect from all those around you, especially from your superiors. Now you have the chance to learn something new. After the initial excitement wears off, new responsibilities can seem overwhelming. There is always a bit of trepidation when venturing into new waters. Try this ritual to help you steer a straight course.

A new position entails new responsibilities. At first those responsibilities may seem heaped upon you with no rhyme or reason. Finding and taking that first step in the right direction is always the hardest thing about a new position. Try to imagine yourself as an explorer in a new land. What two things does every explorer need? Why a map and a compass, of course. Without those, how could anyone ever expect to find his way?

Take a page from an explorer's notebook and buy yourself an inexpensive compass. You can find one at any sporting goods store. Take it to work with you and tack it up on your bulletin board. If that is a little too public for you, then keep it in a desk drawer that you open often. As you are presented with each new item in your new position take a few moments to focus on the compass and ask yourself: "What direction does this task need to take?" Write down your answer.

If no answer is forthcoming, then it's time to consult your map. "What map?" you may ask. Well, the best map in this situation is the person who held the position before you. If he is out of touch, then consult your boss. Trust me, your boss expects you to ask questions about your new position and responsibilities.

Before you know it, you will find your way to the treasure. Even if X doesn't quite mark the spot, if you follow the trail and take it one step at a time you will find your way to the *next* great adventure.

Friday Afternoon (Start of the Weekend)

Many of us already have rituals that signal the start of the weekend, although we may not view them as such. Stopping at the same bar on your way home from work for Margaritas with friends is a ritual if you do it every Friday. So is stopping at the video store every Friday. So, here's a ritual you can begin before you step out of the office door and continue it on your way home. If you commute with others or take public transportation, you may want to wait until you get home for the last part of this ritual. Even if you work at home (as I do) you can do this ritual before leaving your desk. It's fun and a great way to de-stress after a long week.

Upon deciding to leave, take a few minutes to write down the top five "to-do's" for Monday morning. If you don't do this, the most pressing matters at work will tend to bug you all weekend. You need to get them out of your head. You don't have to be extremely detailed, just a few words should do it. There are several positive effects in doing this. First, it gets work priorities out of your head so they won't continue to knock around in there all weekend. Since you leave the list on your desk, you are symbolically leaving the work there as well. That list will be on your desk to help kick-start your Monday morning, reminding you of what needs to be taken care of first thing. It can also remind you of what you were working on Friday afternoon so you can pick up where you left off.

If you're commuting with others, try to guide the conversation away from work on to more recreational topics, such as weekend plans. This gets your mind to switch tracks and actually helps you to relax. It also helps you focus on home improvement projects or family matters so you look forward to getting home. Otherwise you may go on automatic, suddenly looking up and finding that your body is at home, but your thoughts are still at work. If you have no specific plans for the weekend (lucky you!) then discuss other topics with your carpool mates. A few possibilities could include recent movies, foreign countries you've always wanted to visit, or each other's hobbies. Be creative. With practice it gets easier to direct conversations away from stressful topics like work, politics, war, and health care.

If you take public transportation, try to have a novel or some other *enjoyable*, recreational read with you on Friday afternoon. Steer clear of the newspaper in general (except for the comics) and the financial and business sections in particular. Get caught up at another time. Remember, the weekend starts when you *leave the office*.

Now for the fun part. If you're in the car all by yourself, do the following on the way home. Take a deep breath, think of all the frustrations of the week, and scream! You heard me right. Scream. It releases tension. If you are the persuasive type and you carpool, you may be able to convince your carpool mates to do this with you. Who knows, the "Commuters Group Scream" might become the next big trend! If you think your friends would consider you a candidate for the local mental hospital just for suggesting it, then wait until you get home. Then lock yourself in your bathroom, put a pillow over your face, and scream.

If screaming makes you feel too weird or if it would bother those at home, there is another solution. Sigh—heavily. (See the ritual "Coming Home" in chapter 1, "Everyday Stuff," page 1). Releasing your breath with an *audible* sigh relaxes neck and shoulder muscles. The resulting intake of breath is typically deeper, so it oxygenates your blood and further relaxes your muscles. Do this as many times as necessary to fully relax and remember to make a sound when you exhale. That's what makes it work. Your family will love you for it and you will feel ready to start the weekend in a relaxed mood.

The good news? You have left work at the office where it belongs. Enjoy your weekend, and bring on the Margaritas!

Vacation

There's one little word that can brighten every worker's day no matter how overworked he or she feels: *Vacation*. No work, no schedules, no deadlines—just free time to do with what *you* want. But by the time many of us can relax and finally begin to enjoy our vacation, it's almost over. In this country most of us only get a week or two of vacation a year, and a recent trend has been to take lots of three- or four-day weekends instead of one long annual vacation. The problem with that is the vacation *is* practically over before it has truly begun. Whether we take long or short vacations, we need to prepare ourselves. How you spend your vacation is up to you. Whether you decide on a Caribbean cruise, a fishing trip to the mountains, or a stay at home to paint the living room, this ritual will get your vacation off to a good start.

Starting a vacation is a little like leaving work on a Friday afternoon and all the rituals suggested in that section can be expanded a bit for this occasion as well. In addition, you'll want to try one or more of the following.

Find a little time immediately upon getting home from work. Take your briefcase, day planner, or something that represents work to you and *stow it*! Seriously. Find a place out of the way where that symbolic representation of work will not stare you in the face. It could be the top of the closet, in a file drawer, or hidden in the kitchen cabinet. As you do so, say these words.

> *Work is hidden from sight.*
> *It is put away for now.*
> *Out of sight and out of mind.*
> *Now it is vacation time!*

You may want to write yourself a note as to where it is put away, so you can find it again at the end of your vacation.

Next, find a favorite piece of vacation gear and wear it or put it someplace you can see. A hat from Hawaii or a photo of the Grand Canyon or, better yet, a brochure of your destination, if you are traveling, will shift your focus from work to relaxation. Now pack and get out of here, unless of course you're staying home during your vacation.

If your vacation is a home based one it is much more difficult to break from everyday routines. When you are vacationing at home, think of these as short rituals that will help you relax.

Unplug! Really! E-mail can wait and as much as we would like to believe otherwise, it is nearly impossible to only surf. That icon that tells us we have mail is just too annoying to ignore.

Tell friends, family, and especially coworkers that you are going away even if you aren't. Let the answering machine pick up your calls. You can always check your messages so you will know if there is an emergency. Otherwise, they may be tempted to contact you since you will be home anyway. Sometimes, we need vacations, not only from work, but from everything else in our lives also and that includes friends and family.

Don't do anything that is part of your normal habit. Shower in a different bathroom or sleep in the guest room your first night. This will take you out of the everyday routine and make your vacation out of the ordinary.

Whether you're planning an overseas trip or just three days off to paint the living room, whatever you do . . . have fun!

Bon Voyage!

Retirement

My husband has an interesting definition of retirement. He says that retirement doesn't mean you stop doing things or even that you stop working. Retirement is doing what you *want* to do instead of doing what you *have* to do. If you planned well, you will no longer need to earn a living. That doesn't mean, however, that you can't make some extra money doing something that you love, even if it's only a pittance in comparison to your working salary. Smart man, my hubby. I think I'll keep him. Gone are the days when you worked your whole life for the same company, then at retirement you got a gold watch and a pension. I always thought a watch for retirement was an odd gift. Now that you no longer have to follow a schedule, they give you something to keep time. Keep time. Maybe a watch is an appropriate retirement gift after all. This ritual shows you why.

Most of us have some sort of timepiece in our workspace. If you don't, then on your last day of work, make sure that you bring one in with you. It needs to be a clock with an actual face and hands, not a digital one. Don't use your watch, since that is already a personal item. At the end of your workday before going home or to the company bash to celebrate your retirement, take a moment to sit quietly and focus on the clock in front of you. Visualize all the hours that you have worked in your lifetime, then take a pencil and write the words "for others" on the clock face with arrows between the hours of nine and five. It doesn't have to be highly visible.

Next, imagine all the things you will be doing with that time now that you are retiring. Use a permanent marker to overwrite the words "for others" with the words "for me." Keep this clock as a reminder that working for others is now a faint memory and whether you decide to play golf, start your own business, or travel, your time is now your own.

Happy retirement!

The Downs

No, it's not a racetrack, although at times it sure feels like one. Where do you think the term "rat race" came from? When things aren't going well at work—tension, impending deadlines, or layoffs—our fuses become shorter with the people we care about at home. These rituals will help with the downs of work life and hopefully keep the stresses under control and away from your personal life.

Commuting—Stuck in Traffic

I live in Sugar Land, Texas—a nice little community just outside of Houston. I have most everything I need for everyday living: grocery stores, doctors offices, restaurants, movie houses. But when I need anything beyond those basics I have to go "into town." Aaaarrrgggg! The Houston metropolitan area's population is four million people. It is second only to Los Angeles in area, and it has no decent mass transit system. We love our cars here in Texas and that love calls for sacrifices, mainly being trapped in traffic for hours on end. When the traffic is flowing it can still take nearly two hours to drive from one edge of the city to the other. Needless to say, I have developed several small rituals to pass the time while I am trapped in the car. These are especially important to my sanity when the traffic slows to ten miles per hour or, worse yet, stops completely!

Music. It's true what they say: "Music has charms that soothe the savage breast." Music that you love relaxes you. So when you're stuck, turn off the news report and tune into a favorite radio station. Better yet, slip in a favorite CD, so that you won't have to listen to those annoying commercials. It doesn't have to be "soothing" music to relax you, either. As a matter of fact when I'm stuck in traffic, I usually resort to something upbeat like Bon Jovi, Matchbox Twenty, or those good ol' Texas boys ZZ Top. This kind of music lifts my spirits and makes me feel better. So, whether your favorite toe tappin' music is Santana, the Dixie Chicks, or Mary J. Blige, blare it out of your speakers and feel your shoulders begin their migration away from your ears.

Animal likenesses. This ritual only works if the traffic is crawling along or stop-and-go. It would be rather difficult—not to mention dangerous—to look at other drivers if you're tooling along at sixty miles per hour. Anyway, if you're stopped, take a look at the people in the cars around you. Try to figure out what kind of animal they most closely resemble. That big, burly guy in the pickup looks like a bulldog, while the slender blonde in the sports car resembles a gazelle. And you could swear the colorfully dressed little girl who can't seem to sit still is a butterfly or hummingbird. This exercise not only makes the time fly it also stretches your imagination muscles. And it gets more fun the more you do it.

License plates. Another mind stretcher is to try and figure out phrases from the letters of the license plates around you. Again, you can try to match these phrases to the people driving the cars. For example, part of my license plate is YFF and I have translated that into "Years of Fun and Frolic." Seems silly, I know, but who declared that adults can't be silly, anyway?

Silly fun. Speaking of being silly, these last couple of suggestions will not only help keep you from getting annoyed at
the traffic, but they also bring a smile to those around you. I
keep a bottle of children's soap bubbles in my car and when
I'm stopped because of a train or at an exceptionally long
light, I roll down the window and blow them into traffic. Or I
will put my arms out the window and pretend I'm rowing a
boat. The great joy in doing these things comes from seeing
the frowns of people around me being replaced with smiles
and laughter.

Remember, we can't do anything about traffic jams, so
instead of getting annoyed I have one simple piece of advice.
Play!

Monday Morning

Yuk! Nobody likes Monday mornings. Even if you love your
job, Monday morning can hit you like a bucket of cold water.
Why? It's a change in routine, for one thing. We have different
established routines for weekdays and weekends. On Friday,
we're usually looking forward to the next couple of days of
relaxation and play, so the change in routine is a welcome
one. We tend to look forward to sleeping in. But on Monday
we're facing an alarm clock and a week's worth of work.
Hardly exciting. So instead of dreading Monday, try one of
these rituals Sunday night to help get you back into work
mode *before* the alarm goes off the next day.

Think about that top five "to-do" list you left on your desk on
Friday afternoon. Try to re-create it Sunday night, but don't
spend much time on it. It *is* still the weekend, after all. Take

this list with you to work Monday morning. You may find
that the lists don't match, but that's okay. Now you've got a
longer list and you may have remembered details while you
were at home and relaxed that you might have forgotten
otherwise.

Check the weather report, so you can pick out and iron
what you are going to wear the next day. That way you won't
get any rude surprises when you find your favorite blouse or
tie has a spot on it. Or that a cold front came in overnight
and you can't wear what you originally planned to, because
it is no longer appropriate for the weather.

The last thing you want to do before you crawl into bed
is set your alarm. As you do so, say:

> *Play is done.*
> *Monday has come.*
> *Work for five and play for two.*
> *Tomorrow morning,*
> *I won't be blue.*

Now you have set the intent to awake with a good attitude
and you will be better prepared for the work week. So, get to
work.

Work Tensions

Sometimes when tension in the workplace is high it becomes
difficult to concentrate on your job. Some causes may be
rumors of impending layoffs, meetings behind closed doors
that end in grim-faced personnel emerging from within,
silence from upper management, rapidly approaching dead-

lines, shortened work hours, and cutbacks in benefits. The list goes on and on. Whatever the cause of the tension, the following ritual can help you cope. Remember, the situation is usually worse in your mind that it will ever be in reality.

Sit at your desk with your feet flat on the floor. Fold your hands in your lap or let them dangle at your sides. Close your eyes and take a deep breath. Imagine that breath so deep that it actually goes into the ground at your feet. This may be difficult to do with your first breath, but keep trying until you get the hang of it. Once you do, move on to the next step. Imagine roots sprouting from that breath and growing out of the bottom of your feet. See those roots finding purchase in the soil as you say the following (either aloud or to yourself if there are others around):

> *I am safe, stable, and secure.*
> *I am grounded in the earth.*
> *My roots are healthy and strong.*

With your next breath, visualize your body as the trunk of a great tree with branches growing from your arms. Once that picture is clear in your head, say the following:

> *If a storm is approaching, I will bend and sway in*
>   *the winds.*
> *My supple branches will endure and even if some*
>   *break, I will survive.*
> *The storm will pass and new growth will follow.*

Open your eyes and look out through the leaves and feel yourself as the tree.

You have now set the intent to be strong no matter what happens. Whenever you feel overwhelmed by tension, repeating the words is not necessary. Simply imagine yourself as the tree. It may feel strange the first few times, but it really works to relieve tension and anxiety.

Another great tension reliever is laughter. Bring in something small to place on your desk that makes you smile. Arrive early one day and place a piece of candy with an anonymous note that says "Smile," "Relax," or "Play" in everyone's desk drawer. You will feel better and so will your colleagues.

Last, but not least, try to refrain from speculation. Speculation only increases tension. If you can't convince your coworkers to do this, then try to tune out negativity when the speculation starts. The storm will eventually pass, the clouds will break up, and work tensions will evaporate into a clear blue sky.

Reprimand—Demotion

Other than getting fired, one of the most disheartening times in our careers can be the day we receive an official reprimand or a demotion. Sometimes this event blows in out of the blue, but oftentimes, we see it coming. Absenteeism, sloppy work, missed deadlines, work overload—all can contribute to reprimands and demotions. Whether or not you feel a reprimand is deserved, this ritual will help you view it as a positive chance to improve.

Every criticism is an opportunity for growth. With that in mind, gather a nut for every point of negativity included in your reprimand or demotion. For each negative point, use a different nut. These could include acorns from your front yard, as well as pecans or peanuts from your local grocery. Try to find nuts still in their shells since they will be around for a while. Sunflower seeds work exceptionally well, because they are not only small and flat, but they are also abundant and easy to find. Write down each point from your reprimand on a separate piece of paper, then tape a nut below those words. Keep these in your desk or in a small box underneath it.

To break negative habits that could lead to another demotion, or worse, loss of your job, use this visualization every time you are tempted to call in sick when you aren't, to hand in sloppy work, or to procrastinate on a big project.

Remind yourself often of the points of your reprimand. Imagine a piece of that particular nut being eaten away when you are tempted to continue along that destructive path. When you *overcome* that same urge, add another nut to the page.

It is said that it takes twenty-one days to form a new habit or to change an old one. When the nuts on a particular page number twenty-one, take them and scatter them in a favorite park. As you do, imagine a forest of compliments where once stood a nut of criticism.

Losing Your Job

It doesn't matter whether you've been laid off, fired, or quit; losing your job is a serious blow to your self-esteem and self-confidence. Work is so much a part of daily life that losing a job is like losing a member of the family. Some say, "It's only a job. You'll get another one." While others say, "You never liked that job anyway. Now you can find something you really want to do." All true statements. However, grieving must come first. This ritual brings closure and prepares you to move on.

As you gather your belongings from your work area, think about all the good times you had working in this space. With each item you place in your briefcase or box, you are taking home a job well done, a project you received praise for, self-satisfaction, and skills that will be valuable elsewhere. Mentally thank this workplace for providing you with a living while challenging you to achieve your goals. On your way out thank all the people you have worked with, including those with whom you disagreed or had problems. This helps you make a clean break and leave your job with a positive outlook.

Once you arrive home, create a list of all the negatives about your past job. Make this list as complete as possible. Don't worry about being petty, no one else is going to see this list. If you find yourself crying, that's okay. This is a grieving process after all. Read this list to yourself either silently or aloud. By doing this, you are intentionally bringing up the hurt, anger, and pain associated with losing your job. That's a good thing, because now that these emotions are on the surface, it's easier to get rid of them. And the way to do that is by burning the paper. As you burn it, mentally throw those negative emotions into the fire along with the paper. Say the following as you watch the flames:

> I release this job and clear the space in my life
>   for a better one.
> I move beyond negative associations.
> I remember only the good times.
> I will not repeat the mistakes of the past.

After the fire goes out, it's time for the fun part—celebrate. Sounds strange, I know. You are not celebrating the loss of your job, you're celebrating the freedom to find something new and better. *And* you're celebrating all that your previous job has done for you. Have a nice dinner out, go dancing, or invite friends over for a good old-fashioned wake. Whatever way you decide to celebrate, you will find yourself refreshed, clear, and ready for new opportunities.

First Unemployment Check

As if losing a job isn't bad enough, most of us feel funny applying for and receiving unemployment. It may seem that we're getting something for nothing, but that's not the case at all. Unemployment is temporary, and this ritual should help you come to terms with relying on the state to help you out.

Since you will be looking for work while receiving an unemployment check, take a few moments to track your search. Track each phone call you make, every résumé you send, and every person you network with by placing a hash mark on a piece of paper. Label these hash marks as employment "points." For every interview you actually go on, give yourself five points. For every second interview, give yourself ten points.

When you get your first unemployment check, divide the amount of the check by the number of points you have accumulated. What you will be left with is a dollar amount for each effort you have made in your job search. For example, if you have made ten phone calls and have had two interviews that gives you twenty points. If your check is $200 divide that amount by twenty. The result is ten. That means you've been paid ten dollars for each phone call you made and $50 for each interview. So the check is your reward for your job search. This is the only time in your working life that you will want to be paid less for each effort that you make. Try to make that number as small as possible, and you will soon be working again.

Good luck!

Job Search

Most people dread looking for a new job. Posting résumés, making phone calls, networking, and interviewing can really take it out of you. Searching for work can be more of a job than the job itself. This ritual will help you focus on the job you want both before and during your search.

Start with a large piece of poster board and different-color markers. If this makes you uncomfortable or you don't have a space large enough to tack this up, you can use a regular piece of paper and color pens or pencils. A black pen and different-color highlighters would work as well. On the poster board, write all the things you want in a dream job. Get detailed. Choosing the right color enhances different goals, so use the following list to determine the colors you will use.

Green is the color of money, so write a salary range in this bold color at the very top of your chart. It's important to put a range instead of a rock-hard figure. The bottom number should be just slightly above the absolute minimum you need to live. Make the upper number one step beyond what you think the top pay is for the position you are seeking. If you are changing careers and are unsure of what these numbers may be, there are a number of online resources that can help you. This way, you set the intent that it is possible to make the most you can in your chosen profession. Include potential growth and promotional opportunities in this color, too. Remember, you don't want a job you're going to get stuck in. Green is also a good color to use for job titles if you are looking in the health care or financial fields.

Use *red* to list what inspires you in your job. The level of activity and intensity that you wish to be involved with on a daily basis is also a good thing to list in the color red, since it is an active and intense color. If you are a construction worker or perform any kind of physical labor, then use red to write potential job titles.

The social aspects of your job and the amount of imagination and playfulness required should be written in *orange*. If you wish to work independently use this color. Orange is the color you want to use for jobs that are competitive in nature. Job titles written in this color include those that combine physical labor with public interaction—a flight attendant, for example.

Is the type of work you do creative? Then use the *yellow* marker to list potential job titles. This is also a good color to list the lessons you want to learn while doing your job. Use yellow to list the logical aspects of the job, as well. If you want to be able to work at home occasionally or have flexible hours, write these desires in yellow.

Want a job where loyalty is a key issue? Do you manage others? Then write your job title in *blue*. If your job takes vast patience or requires customer contact use this color to list those professions. Customer service representatives, receptionists, telemarketers, and public relations personnel all fall into this category. Future dreams and visions of success should also be written in the color blue.

Calling all executives! *Purple* is your color. The level of power you wish to possess should be written in this color. What inspires you to do your best? Write it in purple!

Don't just write your goals in words, either. Draw pictures, too. Drawing pictures helps awaken the creative side of the brain instead of focusing only on the logical. Add to this list as more ideas strike your brain. You may find yourself crossing things out as well. No matter what, keep in mind that you spend most of your waking hours at your job, so be as detailed as possible. In this ritual, there is no such thing as a trivial line item. If it occurs to you, even if it sounds silly at the time, it is probably a good idea to include it. Post this list somewhere where you can read it often, and good luck in your search.

Shoot for the moon; even if you miss, you'll land among the stars.

The Executive Washroom

When you reach a position of leadership in your career, everything changes, and others will look to you for direction. Now that *you* are the boss, you are responsible for people as well as projects, for morale as well as the annual report. There are the joys of hiring and overseeing work well done. There are the stresses of letting people go and losing customers. This section is for the bosses and business owners whose stresses are different from those of the average worker.

Starting Your Own Business

Starting your own business is exciting, thrilling, and terrifying all at the same time. You no longer have the safety net that being an employee carries with it. *You* are in charge. *You* are the ultimate authority. Every small decision you make affects the business in a big way—especially in the beginning. You've learned from your past experiences and decided that it's time to put your own ideas into play. Starting your own business can be in any industry from manufacturing to retail to service. Becoming an independent contractor in the corporate world can also be considered starting your own business, even if you are the only employee. Ribbon cuttings are fine rituals if you have a storefront; this ritual takes that concept one step further.

Find an empty box. The size doesn't matter, for there will be very little in it to begin with. Decorate the box and its top inside and out. Make it the most beautiful box in the world. This box is all about expectations and prosperity, so use the fanciest paper and the most brilliant color ribbons you can find. Make sure the box can be opened without ripping the paper, for you will be getting into it periodically; therefore, you will need to wrap the top and bottom separately. Don't forget to decorate the inside as well. Place your name or your business name on the front. Include your logo if you have one.

On very nice stationery that complements the wrapping paper, write your expectations for the business. Take your time and include everything you can think of even if it initially seems an impossible goal. Dream big. If not for big dreams, you would have never started your own business to begin with.

The day before you open your doors for business or make your first phone call, place the list inside the box and tie a ribbon around it to hold it closed. On opening day, "cut the ribbon" on your box. Remove the expectation list and read it aloud to all your employees. If your only employee is yourself, go ahead and read it aloud anyway. You are affirming your goals. Set the bar high from the beginning. After reading the list, place it back inside the box.

During the course of doing business, you will reach some of these goals, while others will fall by the wayside. With each goal that you reach, place something representing that goal inside the box. Take those expectations out and read them occasionally, especially when times are rough. On the first-year anniversary of your business, remove everything from the box and review your progress. Reevaluate your goals and write a new list. Make sure you date the list and don't throw out the old one, but place it back in the box as well. Just think what that faded piece of paper will tell you about yourself after you've made your first million!

Redecorate the box when the paper becomes faded or torn. As a representation of your business, you will want to keep it fresh and new. Success!

Hiring

Whether you work for yourself or for someone else, when you're the boss, the fun of hiring is all yours. Making a new employee feel welcome is more than just saying "Welcome

aboard." It's about making that person a part of the organi-
zation and a part of the team. This ritual shows your new
addition how welcome she truly is.

Ask your new employee what her favorite beverage is while
she works. Buy an appropriate container for that beverage. A
mug for coffee, a small glass for juice, an insulated holder
for sodas, a large glass for water—whatever you choose
should be different from everyone else's. It should be something personal and permanent, no paper cups. Personalize
this vessel with your new employee's name or initials.

As the boss it's up to you to determine who will be present for this ritual. It could be the two of you or the entire
department. If your company is small, you could include the
entire workforce in this welcoming ritual.

Present your new employee with the empty vessel and as
you fill it with her favorite beverage say:

May your work here be as sturdy as this cup.
May it never spill or tip over on important documents.
May it always contain tasty treats, never bitter dregs.
May it always be full, but never overflowing.
May it bring you refreshment in its contents,
And camaraderie in its refilling.

This would be a good time to refill and reaffirm all the
employee glasses or just have a toast to the new employee
and end the toast with:

Success!

Firing

Now for the other side of the coin: firing someone; it's never easy. I know of no boss who actually enjoys letting someone go. It feels like a personal failure. There are sleepless nights and lots of trying new things before this tough decision is made. Firing someone because they cannot perform their duties adequately is much different from layoffs or cutbacks due to economics. If you are in this unenviable position, perhaps this ritual will bring you some peace.

By the time you get to the point of actually firing your employee, a great deal of anger may have built up. Anger at your employee, yes, but also anger at yourself for not being able to inspire and motivate that employee. It's best to try and dissipate the anger before you actually do the firing. That way you can be blunt but dispassionate.

The night before you actually fire this person who has aroused your ire, build a monument to him. Do this either at home or behind closed doors. Home is best, since you don't want to be interrupted and you may get loud as well.

Use old cans, building blocks, playing cards, or just folded pieces of paper. You probably have to document why this person is being let go. As you place each new item on the monument, take this document and read off the reasons the employee is being terminated.

After the monument is completely built it is time to vent your frustrations. It's okay, say what you like, there is no one to hear you. Lose your temper. If you choose to use crude language, that's okay, too. Better here and now, than the next day when you are talking to your employee.

As you rant, destroy the monument you built.

While cleaning up the mess, focus on the things *you* could have done better. This puts you in the position of straightening things out and sweeping away old, dead matters.

The next day, as you talk with your employee, picture the monument surrounding him and know that after he walks out the door, the mess can be cleaned up and you can start fresh.

Closing Your Business

It is always a sad day when you decide to close a business you started. It can be like losing a member of the family. Unfortunately, it's all too easy to focus on all the things you did wrong that caused the demise of the business. That's okay if they are constructive negatives that you can learn from. The tendency, however, is to *only* look at the negatives. This ritual will get you past those and help you remember the good times as well.

You will need two inexpensive wineglasses, a bottle of champagne or sparkling cider, a hammer, and an old towel you can throw away.

Set a date to make your closing phone call, provide your final service, or turn in your last project. When that is done, find a quiet place for remembrances and to grieve.

Pour your first glass but don't drink it. As you watch the bubbles float to the surface think of all the things in your business that you could have done better. Focus on the projects that went wrong or the customers you lost. Imagine each of those mistakes as a bubble in the glass. See each one come to the surface and pop. As it pops visualize the hurt

and regret popping with it. Take your time. When it feels like
you have reached the end of this recrimination, take the
glass in hand and pour out the contents. Pour them either
down a drain or into a large body of water. As you pour, say
these words:

> *All mistakes, regrets and poor judgment flow*
> *from my life as this wine flows from this glass.*
> *They are no more.*

Set that glass aside for now and fill the other one. This
glass and its contents represent all the positive aspects of
your business. All the things you did right. All the accomplishments and the lessons you learned along the way. The
invaluable business contacts and friends you made. All these
things are present in the bubbles reaching for the top.
Remember these as you slowly sip the champagne. Refill
your glass if you find it empty before you have finished
counting your blessings. Before you take the final sip, say:

> *This business filled my life with happy times and*
>   *great accomplishments.*
> *May the lessons learned always be with me.*

After you finish the contents wrap both glasses in the
old towel, take the hammer, and smash the glasses as you
say these words:

> *As I break this glass, I break from the past*
>   *and start anew.*

Now, on with your life.

7

Ka-Ching!

PERSONAL FINANCE

MONEY. This is something in our lives that calls for rituals! We give a lot of thought to major purchases, but what about other financial dealings in our lives? Opening a checking account is just as important as getting a raise. Applying for and receiving a credit card can have almost as much impact as buying a home. Even paying bills every month is cause for a celebration. That's right, I said celebration. Read on to find out why. Rituals surrounding all of these money issues and more are included in this chapter.

Opening a Checking Account

The main purpose for opening a checking account is so you can have a steady stream of money that is easily accessible without having to carry cash all the time. With today's debit cards that are used like credit cards, it becomes even easier and more convenient to access your money. The biggest problem can be keeping tabs on that money. You want to be sure that the next time you turn on the tap, something will come out of the faucet. This ritual can be done for an existing account or for a new one.

First of all, think of the term *in the black* when ordering your new checkbook cover or debit card. Fancy designs or specialty checks are okay as long as the colors are subdued and cool. Stick with black, green, or blue for the cover. Black obviously, because of the previous saying. Green is the color of money, so, it, too, is highly appropriate. Blue is the color of water, which can remind us to keep the money flowing. Water designs are also good for the checks themselves. Stay away from reds, oranges, and yellows. These colors are very active and encourage spending.

Before you deposit it, take a few moments and hold on to the cash or check you will be using to open your account. While you hold it visualize a vast lake being present in the money. This is your reservoir. Once you receive your new checkbook, checks, and debit card take a few moments to hold on to them as well, but this time visualize a pipe leading from that reservoir to a faucet you can turn on or off. The checks and debit cards are that faucet. Before you use them for the first time, say the following:

> *Money shows*
> *In my hands* [the checks and debit cards]
> *In and out it goes*
> *With these tools*
> *Here's hoping it flows*
> *With ease*

Each time you make a deposit, imagine rain falling on your lake and raising the water level. With each check you write or debit transaction you make, visualize turning on that faucet. Know that every time you do the level in your lake is dropping.

Here's wishing you a very wet climate. May you never experience a drought.

Opening a Savings Account

Opening a savings account is more exciting than opening a checking account, because it means you have extra money! That's always a good thing, especially in this day and age. Savings accounts serve a variety of functions. You could open an account in order to save money for a new car. Down payments for a variety of things including a house or future college expenses are best accrued outside of your checking account. You might need to put money aside to pay taxes later on. Whatever the reason, it always feels good to have money set aside for a specific reason. Unlike investing (see "Making Investments," page 162), a savings account is short term, although it is a way to invest in your future since you will be using cash instead of credit for major purchases or emergencies. For example, a medical savings account can cover what your insurance doesn't and that kind of account can be tax-deferred! (Check with your company benefits specialist.) This ritual takes the idea of the lake from the previous ritual, "Opening a Checking Account," and expands on it.

The same color rules apply to your savings account register as they did to your checking account and checks. Usually, you take money from checking to open a savings account, or you may acquire a "windfall"—anything from a bonus to a tax refund—that you can save. Take hold of the money that you plan to deposit into your savings account. If it is coming from your checking account, it has to come from your reservoir (the lake we created in the last ritual). Imagine diverting a stream away from that lake. It won't be easy, because we will be sending it uphill. Pump it far up into the mountains, then dam it there and turn it into a glacial lake. Since you don't want this money to flow as freely as the money in your checking account, you are freezing it in place. Whenever you are tempted to remove money from your savings for a frivolous reason, invoke the image of the ice. The longer it sits there the more frozen it becomes. You will need to install a heater and a pipe, so you can thaw it out and transfer it back into your checking account "lake" as needs be.

When transferring future monies *to* the glacier (savings account) say the following:

> *This money is frozen in place.*
> *It will thaw in the future when the spring arrives*
> *The summer of purchases will bring growth to the*
> *   lower fields,*
> *And joy to my life.*

Visualize any interest payments that accrue as gentle snows falling on your frozen lake and increasing it in size.

Good luck, and remember to always pay yourself first. If the money is gone from your check register, it is less tempting to spend it.

May global warming never come to your mountaintop!

Paying Bills

Most of us look forward to paying bills about as eagerly as we look forward to going to the dentist. The difference, however, is the item being extracted. It can be depressing to see our checking account balance shrink as the stack of paid bills grows larger. I'm proposing a radical idea that just may make paying bills a little less onerous—at least to our psyches. Bills are something to be grateful for. This ritual shows you why.

Most of us set aside one evening every week or every couple of weeks to take care of the depressing activity of paying bills. On the evening you have set aside, pour yourself a glass of water, grab a snack from the fridge or pantry, pick up a pen and a notepad, and open up the checkbook.

With each bill you pay, you are either going to write down the following affirmations on the notepad in front of you, or say them aloud. Remember, say these with meaning and really think about what you are saying.

I pay these bills with ease and I am grateful for everything they provide.

Mortgage/Rent: *I am thankful for the roof over my head and the walls that keep me safe, warm, and sheltered.*

Cable/Satellite: *I am grateful for the entertainment and stress relief provided by this service, because it helps me relax after a hard day's work. I am also* *grateful for the way it keeps me informed and educated.*

Phone: *The connectedness I have with the community at large and family and friends in particular is worth more than the amount I am paying for this service.*

Electric: *I can keep my food and drinks fresh and my air cooled in the summer because I have this bill.*

Natural Gas: *As I pay this bill, I am grateful for the warmth provided in the cold of winter and the hot water with which I wash.*

Water/Groceries: *I am grateful for the necessities of life provided by this money I pay out.*

Sewer/Trash: *To carry away and treat our waste keeps us clean and in good health. I am thankful that someone else provides me with this service.*

Lawn maintenance/Landscaping: *To arrive home and be greeted with a manicured lawn is a refreshing sight. As I pay this bill, I am grateful that I do not have to toil in the heat.*

Gasoline: *With this bill I pay I realize I can go almost anyplace I can dream about.*

Credit cards (department store, etc.)**:** *From clothes to cookware to linens, I am thankful for the opportunity to provide for my household as I pay this bill with ease.*

Medical/Life insurance: *I am thankful I can provide myself and my family peace of mind for the unfortunate times of crisis in our lives.*

Taxes: *I am grateful for the structures this bill provides: roads, schools, and the countless other services that my government supplies.*

If you do this ritual every time you pay bills, I guarantee that your perception of bills will change and it will no longer be such an onerous task. In addition, you will become more grateful for the basics and the extras in your life. You may be paying out your hard-earned money, but you are receiving something in return. This ritual makes you more aware of that.

Bills are a sign of abundance!

New Credit Card

Receiving your first credit card is like adopting a two-headed dog. One head is always licking your hand, encouraging you to pet it. It brings you your slippers and your newspaper and lays its head in your lap or sits quietly at your feet. The other head shreds your newspaper, bites you on the butt, and is constantly growling or barking. The trap is that the loyal dog can turn against you as well, if you ignore its brother for too long. With credit, it's important to establish good habits immediately. It is all too easy to get ourselves in trouble. We tend to ignore the warning growls in favor of the wonderful loyalty given us. This ritual will help you to realize that the definition of credit is that someone trusts you enough to give you an advance to buy what you want now, instead of having to wait and save for it.

* * *

You will need a bag of rocks, a stack of play money, and a large jar, box, or basket. Using the play money, count out what amounts to approximately five to six weeks of salary. It's best if you use small denominations. How small those denominations are is determined by the amount of money you make. (Fives are a little too small if your monthly salary is over several thousand.) You can get play money at your local toy store or you can make your own on the computer. If you do print your own, make sure it is sufficiently different from what our currency actually looks like or it could be considered counterfeiting. Now, place it in the jar.

Every time you charge something on your new credit card remove that amount of play money from your jar and replace it with the same number of rocks. If it's an odd number, always round up. The rocks represent your debt load. When you make a payment, take out the rocks and put the money back in—minus the amount of interest you are paying.

If the jar is ever completely empty of money and full of rocks, it's time to stop using your card for a while, until you can empty out some of those rocks. It's a general rule of thumb that your debt load (minus a mortgage) should *never* exceed ten percent of your annual salary. That's five to six weeks worth of pay, the amount of money you first put in the jar.

This ongoing ritual should help keep you on track with your credit card and give you a visual representation of your debt. It should also help you to prevent having to perform the final ritual in this chapter, "Filing Bankruptcy."

Keep both those dogs happy and they will provide you with years of loyalty and contentment.

New Mortgage

Buying a home—wow, what a rush! After all the papers have been signed and the keys are in your hand, walking in the front door of your new home is quite thrilling. You can paint the walls any color you want, change the bathroom fixtures, or replace that awful blue carpet with beautiful hardwood floors. You can do whatever you want and there's no one to tell you otherwise. Along with the freedom to decorate and change the house in any way you want comes the downside of home ownership—the broken pipes in the middle of the night, roofs that need mending, and yards to mow. You can no longer just call the apartment complex or condo association to have something fixed. Owning a house definitely has its financial ups and downs. This ritual celebrates the sweet and compensates the sour of home ownership.

The experts estimate that a house will need repairs and upkeep to the tune of 1 percent of the worth of the house per year. Speaking from experience, it's usually all at once. It can be quiet for a couple of years with only a little new paint or a faulty door handle. Then—*pow*—the hot water heater melts down, the dishwasher starts spewing forth suds, and the ceiling fan shorts out, all in the same month! The idea is to have a savings account in which you slowly set aside emergency house repair funds. You can do the ritual "Opening a Savings Account" (page 152) for those contingencies. So much for the sour, now for the sweet.

Purchase a dollhouse—either unfinished from the local craft shop or a used one from a garage sale. You may even find one haunting your attic. However you obtain it, start out this ritual with a fresh coat of white paint on the outside of the dollhouse.

Using a pencil, create a grid over that fresh paint. The number of squares can be determined in one of two ways. There can be the same number of squares as there are months or years in your mortgage. As you make each payment paint in one of those squares. Use whatever color feels good to you. If you are painting in squares on a monthly basis, you could use a different color for each year. There's nothing to stop you from painting a different color for every month if you like. It sure will end up being an interesting patchwork if you do. This exercise gives you a solid representation of just how much of your house you own. If you make double payments, paint accordingly. If you refinance, you'll have to start all over again with the white paint.

Keep this model in a place where it will regularly remind you of how lucky you are to be in your own home.

Welcome to the roller-coaster ride, and have fun!

Getting a Raise

It's an exciting day when you get a raise. It is such a positive affirmation of a job well done that it definitely deserves a ritual. Promotions, time served, that extra effort, even cost-of-living increases—all are reasons to celebrate. Before performing this ritual, you need to decide what you are going to do with that extra money. Will it go into your regular everyday income? Are you lucky enough to be able to invest it long term? Or will you put it in savings for a specific future purpose? Once you have made this decision, do this ritual to reaffirm it.

* * *

You will want to set your intent for the extra money with the first paycheck in which your raise appears. So do with it what you have planned. Put it in your savings account, invest it, or use it to pay bills. Remember, you are establishing what will eventually become a habit.

The extra money in your *next* paycheck you will get to have some fun with. Take the amount of the raise and buy something completely frivolous—something you would not normally buy. Even with as little as ten dollars, you can have some fun. You can purchase a new DVD or CD that you wouldn't buy otherwise or have lunch at a restaurant if you normally brown-bag it at work. With larger amounts, you could take a weekend trip or spend the night in a fancy hotel with room service. You could buy that home stereo system you've always wanted or a luxury sheet set.

Whatever you decide to spend your money on, buy your special item with the knowledge that it is your reward for a job well done.

You deserve it!

Giving to Charity

In some religions, giving to charity is required. It's called tithing, which basically means you give a tenth of what you have to those less fortunate. Giving to charity must be something that comes from the heart and it must also be something you can afford. You don't have to give monetarily either, you can give of yourself and of your time. Helping to build homes for the poor, donating outgrown clothing or other items that you no longer have any use for are ways to give to charity. Visiting a homebound elderly person for an hour a week not only makes that person feel good, it will make you feel good, too. It also sets a good example for others. Whatever you give, this ritual can be done each time you give of your time, your money, or your self. It is built around the idea of a tithing, but not as a requirement.

After you have written a check or performed a service for charity, the obvious reward for you is a feeling of contentment. You feel good about yourself for doing something for someone else with no expectation of anything in return. Unless, of course, you can deduct your gift. Sounds crass, I know, but why should it? It shouldn't, of course. We live in a society where we expect returns on our investments, so why should charity be any different?

Take the time to think about what kind of return that you personally will receive from your charitable acts. It could be anything from a tax deduction to a clean closet. But I want you to think bigger, deeper. Think about the benefit to society that will eventually affect you.

For example, let's say you work in a soup kitchen once a month. This feeds others, but how does it feed you? Some politicians like to talk about the trickle-down effect—if those at the top have more they will give more. What I'm talking about is the trickle-up effect—by giving more to those at the bottom, what benefit comes up the ladder?

If a person has a full belly and doesn't have to worry about where his next meal is coming from, what might he be able to do instead? If a schoolchild has an after-school program to attend, will that make her a better citizen in the long run? What if, in one of those programs, the child discovers that she likes science? She might end up becoming a doctor or medical researcher and saving lives!

Asking yourself these questions can become a ritual in every aspect of your life. Eventually you will end up giving more. Instead of seeing destitute homeless people or impoverished kids, you will begin to see human beings with potential to grow. When we are the recipients of charity we tend to give back when we are able. By giving, we are helping to create more givers. That's something to think about.

Keep these things in mind the next time you are asked to give to charity and watch it "trickle-up!"

Making Investments

You are taking an active role in long-term planning for your life when you make investments. Investing in real estate, the stock market, or an up-and-coming business or product is often risky. You never know how it will turn out in the long run. But you make that investment hoping to increase its value years down the line and walk away with much more than you put in. It takes money, yes, but it also takes an investment of time, time in which you are waiting and not doing. This ritual will make the waiting a little more bearable and help you to see progress, however slow it may be.

You will no doubt be tracking your investment daily, weekly, monthly, or even yearly. Even so, you're only seeing numbers on a page, and it's sometimes hard to judge how well you're really doing. So I'm going to give you something concrete to focus on.

Build a set of stairs or a ladder. It can be just a graph on a piece of paper if you like, but that's not nearly as much fun as having an actual staircase in front of you.

Go to your local craft or hobby shop and buy a bag of craft sticks and a bottle of glue. Make the stairs ten steps tall to begin with. I hope you will be adding more later. Write the name of the investment on the side of the stairs, like *XYZ Stock* or *Property at 1234 Main Street*.

Next, find something to represent your investment. It could be an actual piece of money like a dollar coin or a roll of pennies. You might want to use a seed to represent growth or a doll to represent yourself. If you are simply using a graph on paper, you will need to tape your token to the page, so make it sturdy.

After making the initial investment, place your token on the second to the bottom step. You will never go below the bottom step unless you either lose everything or cash out on your investment. Decide how much your investment must increase or decrease in value in order to move up or down a step. The change can be large or small, it's your choice. Write the dollar amount or percentage number on the step itself. Make the number on the bottom step a number just above your absolute lowest tolerable return. If it goes below that, you will cash out. The top step should contain either the actual number or percentage increase that is your ultimate attainable goal.

Over the course of your investment you will probably be moving both up and down the stairs. Add more steps if you find yourself exceeding your highest expectations. Whatever those may be, you will be able to see at a glance how you are doing.

Your future is brighter for taking risks. No matter what the investment, it is always an investment in your future.

May your stairs always lead up!

Paying Off Your Mortgage

When you pay off your mortgage you gain an enormous amount of freedom. You no longer have to worry about a roof over your head. You are secure in your home and it is now owned *entirely* by you. Wow. Your mortgage payment is typically the largest outgo of the month. How wonderful it is to only have to pay for food and utilities. What to do with that money that no longer has to be paid out is a huge decision and one that should not be made in haste. In the meantime, this ritual celebrates having your home entirely to yourself.

One of the most common ways to celebrate paying off a mortgage is to have a mortgage-burning party. I suggest you take that idea one step further. Throw a party and invite all your friends and family. Have two big bowls with pieces of paper and lots of pens. In one bowl, put red pieces of paper. In the other, provide green paper.

During the course of the party, have the guests write down, on the red pieces of paper, all the negatives they can think of that are associated with having a mortgage. Encourage them to go beyond the obvious aspect of simply making the payment. These can be weighty, like having to deal with lots of different companies throughout the years as banks merge and the actual house note gets bought and sold. Or they can be silly, like no more paper cuts from the checks you've had to write once a month or no more inkstains on your fingers. Tell them to have fun with this and be as silly or serious as they like.

On the green pieces of paper, have your loved ones write down suggestions for what to do with that extra money. Again, these can be serious or silly. Tell them there is no limit to the number of ideas they can suggest. The suggestions can be elaborate, like taking an around-the-world cruise, or simple, like putting money away for retirement. Join your guests in providing suggestions and have fun. This is a party, after all.

At the height of the party, have everyone bring their red pieces of paper to a central location, preferably next to the fireplace or a fireproof container. It could even be a barbecue pit or fire ring in the backyard. Have each person read his paper aloud and then one by one, pitch them into the fire. Give a cheer for each one. Follow this by burning either the original note or a representation of it. Give the biggest cheer of all or sing a song.

After the burning, sit down and read aloud from the green papers. I'm sure you will all be rolling with laughter and crying with joy at all the suggestions.

Enjoy your home, now that it is all yours, and have fun with the money that is no longer required to provide you with shelter.

Welcome home!

Filing Bankruptcy

Ouch! Filing for bankruptcy not only hurts your financial situation, but it is also a big blow to your pride and self-esteem. It takes a while to bounce back. Perhaps this ritual will be the first step on a new path of fiscal responsibility and help ease the pain of this rather difficult transition.

If you have a large chalkboard or white board, do this ritual using one or the other. If you don't own either, and don't wish to buy one, you can do this ritual on your computer or even on a large piece of paper, or poster board.

Divide the board into three sections with the middle section twice as wide as the end sections. In the first section write down all the negative repercussions of making such a decision (low credit rating, diminished purchasing power). The middle section is for all the debts that will be included in the bankruptcy. Fill the last section with all the emotional downs associated with filing bankruptcy. These could include feelings of worthlessness, depression, or anger. Be very specific in these lists. Take your time and write down everything you can think of. Leave this list up for an entire week before your court date. Read it often. You may find yourself adding to it nearly every day.

After the court date, come home and read the middle section, the section listing the debts. Then erase *that* section only. Read your first entry under negative repercussions, then in the middle section write a practical activity that will help you to eventually erase that negative consequence. Next, go to the emotional downs section and read the first line. Think of something that will help you get over that— more time spent with friends, perhaps. Write down that action in the middle section, also.

Go back and forth between the two. Pretty quickly, the middle section will be completely filled with positive actions you can take to help you through this hard time. Leave this list up for as long as you wish. Read it often. Do the activities listed in the middle section and, before you know it, the sting of filing bankruptcy will lessen. You'll soon find yourself enjoying life again and reestablishing your credit and good reputation.

Good luck.

8

Let's Get Physical

HEALTH AND FITNESS

DIET, EXERCISE, SPORTS—sound like great themes for a ritual. These important events in our lives require an enormous amount of focus and concentration if you are going to achieve your goals. There is definitely a need to celebrate winning your first 5k or losing those ten pounds you put on during the holidays. Before you put on workout clothes or climb onto that scale, ritualize your goals with the suggestions from this chapter.

Change in Eating Habits

Diet is a four-letter word! *Diet* has such a negative connotation in our society that I prefer not to use it. Besides, the phrase *on a diet* implies a transitory condition, something we do only for a short period and then head back to "normal" eating habits—a diet to lose extra pounds put on during the holidays, for example. A change in eating habits, however, implies a permanent condition. You can change those habits to lose weight, but you can also change them to improve health conditions such as diabetes, high cholesterol, and hypertension. No matter what program you follow or if you decide to change your eating habits on your own, you need to prepare yourself mentally and emotionally before you begin. You will be putting your body through physical changes. It is always a good idea to consult with your doctor before beginning any exercise routine or diet. Even though this ritual is designed to effect a permanent change in your eating habits, it can be applied to the temporary kind as well. This ritual uses the four elements of Nature to help you in your quest.

Gather representations of each of the four elements. Try to find something as personal as possible. For Air it could be a feather, a set of wind chimes, or a photo of a butterfly. That picture of you as a kid flying a kite would be perfect!

The best representation for Fire would be a red candle, preferably of the pillar type, for you will be lighting it often. If you wish, choose a scented one, but try to stay away from food fragrances like cinnamon, apple, or strawberry. You are trying to change your eating habits, after all, and reminding yourself of food in your ritual is not a good idea. Place a photo of you in front of a vibrant sunrise or sunset to accentuate the power of fire.

The representation for Water could be a shell you picked up from a favorite beach, or a pretty blue bottle filled with tap water.

A potted plant is the best representation of Earth. If you have a black thumb, then use a dish of salt or that rock you found while hiking in the mountains.

Before beginning your "diet" sit down in the kitchen with all of the elemental representations. Find a space in your kitchen where you can keep these items indefinitely. Create a shrine to your good health. Concentrate on each element in turn with the words appropriate for that element.

Start with Air, for Air represents your mental state and your goals. As you concentrate on your Air symbol, say:

> *Air clears my mind and blows away all*
> *impediments to attaining my goals.*

Move next to Fire, for Fire is the courage and inspiration to reach those goals. As you light the candle say:

> *The light of Fire inspires me and gives me*
> *courage to burn away all old eating habits.*

Shift your focus to Water, for Water keeps us emotionally balanced and clean. As you focus on your Water symbol, say:

> *This Water washes away all my fears and*
> *cleanses my body of all impurities.*

Look to Earth last, for Earth represents our physical bodies and the stability of the ground beneath our feet. As you contemplate the Earth symbol, say:

> *Earth keeps me steady on my path and gives me*
> *strength in reaching my goals.*

It's a good idea to do this ritual every morning for a while. As your new habits form, repeat this ritual only as needed. Keep these elements in the kitchen as a constant reminder of your goal. Whatever you do, do *not* keep an unflattering photo of yourself on the fridge. This only accentuates the negative, and it's best to stay positive. Put your goals there instead.

May good health and happiness be yours!

Start of Exercise Program

Congratulations, you've decided to get in shape! What a great affirmation of life! Consider how many quality hours you are adding to your life by taking care of your body. You will have more energy for the things you love: time spent with loved ones, hobbies, or just relaxing. These are extra special hours, for you will be in better health while you are enjoying them. I offer this ritual to help you visualize those extra hours, especially when the task of exercising becomes onerous.

You will need a jar four inches in diameter, large bag of one-inch marbles, pen, and pad. Before you begin your new exercise routine, write down your top five reasons for beginning this exercise program—weight loss, inch loss, toning, increased energy, etc. Make them reasonable and attainable. Be specific. Write down the number of pounds or inches you want to lose or the endurance level you wish to reach. An all-day hike in the mountains without being exhausted is a good example of the type of goal that is hard to define. It doesn't matter whether these are long-term or short-term goals, for you will be changing them periodically. On a separate piece of paper, write down your measurements and weight. Place both these lists underneath the jar and forget about them.

It's important that you do not measure and weigh every

day. Doing so will only dishearten and discourage you. You will be weighing and measuring only when you reevaluate your goals.

On the day you start your new exercise routine, place three marbles in the jar. One is for actually working out, the other two are a bonus for starting. Each time you work out, place one marble in the jar. Visualize each of those marbles as an extra added hour of healthy living. Once the entire bottom of the jar is covered, review your goals. Are you on your way? Weigh yourself and take new measurements. If you haven't made some progress, you may want to reevaluate what you are doing in the way of exercise and increase the level of activity or the frequency. Chances are, though, that you will be able to detect some improvement.

How quickly you manage to cover the bottom of that jar will tell you a great deal as well. If it takes more than two months, you are not working out often enough to make a difference. If you cover it in three to six weeks, you should be able to see the results in your body.

Write down new goals and your new weight and measurements and place them back under the jar. Now it's reward time. Remove one marble and spend an entire hour doing something *you* want to do. Watch television for an hour on a Saturday afternoon, sunbathe in the backyard, or get lost in a novel. If you choose to eat an ice cream sundae, that's okay, too. This is a reward, after all.

Continue putting a marble in the jar each time you exercise. When you fill another level, take away one marble and review goals, take measurements, and reward yourself again. Do this for every layer in the jar. To distinguish between layers as you fill the jar, you might want to make each layer a different color.

For even more incentive to continue your routine, take away one marble for each week you miss. This will keep you moving toward your goals and your new healthy lifestyle. Before long, those pounds will drop off and you will start to feel healthier and more alive.

Feel the burn!

Fresh Appearances

Every once in a while we all need a change. Some of these changes are temporary or easily reversible. We get tired of the same old hairstyle. Ladies, maybe it's time to see a professional makeup artist for a fresh new look. Then there are the more drastic changes that require much more thought. These permanent changes range from tattoos to permanent eyeliner or lip liner, all the way through to plastic surgery. Whether you are cutting your waist-length hair into a short bob or bobbing your nose, changes in personal appearance can be subtle or dramatic. What better time for a ritual? This two-part ritual will take you from before to after.

Before

Before you make the change in appearance, you will want to document the way you currently look. It's a little like a home improvement project. How can you tell there has been an improvement if you don't have pictures to prove it? So, take a photo of what you are going to change about yourself and make two copies. Put one away for future reference. The second copy is yours to play with. If you are going to cut your hair, color out the sections of your hair that will be gone. Changing the color of your hair or getting it streaked? Get those markers out. Even though it will not be a totally accurate picture of the final change, the act of making the change on the photo will mentally prepare you to go through with it.

After

Take a picture with the changes made and compare the before and after photos to see how close they are. Have a good laugh and then throw away the altered "before" photo. Get out the unchanged before photo and compare before and after. If you don't like the changes, go ahead and keep the after photo anyway. It will become your new *before* photo when you go back to the spa or when the haircut grows out.

If you like the change and you keep a photo album, paste both photos side by side with the words "before" and "after." Add comments to the page such as "Wow," "What a babe!" and "Hey, Good Looking." If you don't keep albums then do this on a small piece of poster board and decorate it appropriately.

The last thing you should do is celebrate your new look by drawing attention to it. Buy a beautiful new hair ornament, fresh makeup, or a new blouse taking into account what it is you've had done. Go out and show off your new look to friends. Revel in the attention and compliments generated by your new look. You've created a whole new attitude to go with your new look.

Congratulations, you gorgeous thing, you!

Learning a New Sport

Does the thought of learning how to play baseball excite you? What about hang gliding? Mountain biking can be fun, and so can backpacking, if you want to see those same mountains at a little slower pace. If you have decided to learn something new, no matter what your age, my hat's off to you. Learning a new sport can be thrilling, but it can be intimidating as well. With that in mind, I offer the following ritual to provide the courage to leap into a new game.

Choose an animal, a fish, or a bird that you would most like to be associated with for your new sport. Select a specific type instead of a broad species.

For example, if you're learning to dive, surf, or swim, you could choose a dolphin, whale, otter, or salmon instead of just a "fish." Dolphins are not only swift, but playful and social; they love jumping and riding the waves. Whales are slower, but every move is filled with purpose, and they sing while they swim. Sounds like pure enjoyment to me. Otters are truly caring of their young, so if you're learning to swim because you want to join your children, choose otter. Salmon is all about growth and regeneration, so if you are swimming for health reasons, Salmon might be a good choice for you.

For the more competitive team sports such as baseball, football, soccer, or hockey, choose animals that are fierce. Lions, and tigers, and bears, oh my. Why do you think sports teams are so often named after these fierce predators? Not just because they need an emblem, but because, psychologically, the players take on the aspects of these animals.

If the sport you are learning is one that calls for speed

and solitude, such as running or cycling, choose the cheetah or jaguar—or another animal that is swift yet graceful.

Hang gliding, flying, or skydiving? For hang gliding, try a bird that floats effortlessly. A hawk would be a good choice. The majestic eagle soars above the rest, so if you're learning to fly you might choose this regal bird. Skydiving is not really flying, but it sure feels like it, so a bird is still appropriate. The falcon would work well here for it is a bird that plummets toward the ground at amazing rates of speed, then snaps open its wings and lands gently. Definitely something to keep in mind while skydiving.

Pick one of the creatures I have recommended, or choose another one that's fitting. Do a little research into its habits and traits. Keep this info in a file and read it periodically to remind you of the way you wish to be in your new sport. Acquire a representation of your mascot and throw it in with your gear. Catching a glimpse of a photo or stuffed animal of your choosing while preparing for your sport will help overcome any trepidation you feel. A simple, quick ritual, but one that works well.

Play ball!

First Competition

Once you've reached a certain level of proficiency in a sport, you may choose to compete. Someone from the company softball team may ask you to join. Or you may wish to test your hang-gliding landing skills in an organized contest. Maybe competing in a swim meet or 5k is something you wish to experience. This ritual is to remind you that, although it may appear otherwise, the only person you are truly competing against is yourself.

You've trained and prepared for your first competition and the big day is almost here. On the night before take some time to be alone. But don't use that time to just sit alone and think. That's a surefire way to increase rather than decrease your anxiety. So, I suggest you have a deck of cards with you wherever you decide to spend your quiet time. Give yourself at least an hour to be alone and play solitaire. That's right, I said play solitaire.

As you play, imagine that each card is one aspect of your training and preparation and that each game is a separate competition. You see, although there will be others in the contest, they are all playing with different decks. Some of them have older decks and some, newer. Their cards could stick together or be worn and faded from use. They could be grand master champions of solitaire or only beginners. There are also many versions of solitaire, and their games could be slightly different from the one you are playing. No one has a deck or set of skills identical to yours. You can admire those with better skills and watch and learn from them, but you cannot be the same. The best you can do is play to the best of your ability with the deck that you have been given. Sometimes you'll play the game better than everyone else and other times you won't.

As you round the last bend or finish the final inning, try to keep one thing in mind: It's all in the cards!

Winning and Losing

In sports competitions, as in life, we have both winning and losing moments. The feeling of elation when we win is in itself a ritual and celebration. But losing is another story. Nobody wants to lose, but sometimes it happens. Did you drop the ball or stumble on the final turn? Or was there simply someone more skilled than you? The reason really doesn't matter. What does matter is the lesson learned from the experience and how it can make you better next time. This ritual takes the sting out of losing and allows you to see it as the path to winning.

You will need a piece of poster board, a pencil, and a marker for this ritual. Use the pencil to draw a mountain, covering the poster board top to bottom. This mountain represents the sport in which you are participating. Label it with that sport or attach photos of people you admire that are ace players.

The first time you play competitively take the marker and draw a one-inch line up the side of the mountain. The next time you play, whether it is practice or competition, draw a horizontal line. Alternate directions every time you play: Go either up the mountain or across it. Do this until you win your first competition. By this time you should be pretty far up the mountain. Ever heard the expression that a learning curve is straight up when you begin something? Climbing this mountain is your learning curve.

You will keep moving up the mountain until you have your first win; then if you continue on a winning streak, you will actually be going sideways on the mountain, for you have hit a plateau where your skills have leveled off. Now the next time you lose, start climbing again. For each win, draw a horizontal line and for each loss, a vertical one. When you lose, you are actually learning more than when you win. It is by learning from your losses that you will actually reach the top of the mountain. Winning feels good, but it does nothing for improving your skills.

By the time you reach the top of this particular mountain, you should be fairly proficient in your chosen sport. When that happens, erase the penciled-in mountain and take a good look at the trail you have blazed for yourself. You now have the skills to continue playing and possibly (after completing another mountain or two of the same size) of achieving the proficiency necessary to teach the sport. Remember, the closer you get to the top, the steeper the climb. But the view is definitely worth it. Now, go on to the next mountain, which is even higher than the one you just climbed. The entire range lies before you.

Climb on!

A Visit to the Doctor

Doctor's appointments are rarely any fun. Surrounded by sick people, you sit in a waiting room and try not to breathe in the germs of the people around you. Or *you* could be the sick one, sitting there not wanting to pass on that illness to anyone else. Or you could be there for something simple like a checkup, physical, or drug test for a new job. Whatever the reason, most people hate going to the doctor. Besides the time spent in the waiting room (which sometimes seems interminable) there are other stresses. What if the doctor tells you that something is seriously wrong? Fear is the main reason many people put off going to the doctor even when they have symptoms or problems. Let's change that thought to: "The doctor will give me a clean bill of health." Even if the worst is discovered, the sooner you know the better your chances of recovering. Try this ritual to help you confront and calm your fears and get a better grasp on your situation.

You can do this ritual either while you are waiting in the doctor's office or before you leave home. There are advantages to both. If you do it while you are in the doctor's office, it will help pass the time as well as give you something to focus on instead of the people around you. Having a focus helps to decrease the amount of fear and anxiety you may feel. If you do it at home, you may have more time for the specifics that this ritual calls for; therefore you will have a more complete picture of your problem to present to the doctor. Whichever you decide, the ritual is the same.

Find a line drawing of a person in black and white, like something you would find in a coloring book. It needs to be without such extras as elaborate clothing or fancy backgrounds. If you can't find one, or if you are so inclined, you can draw a simple outline of yourself. Make it basic—head, body, legs, arms, hands, feet. If a specific area is bothering you, spend more time and draw that area in detail. Make several copies of this unaltered drawing, because you will be using more of them as time passes.

Next, take a box of crayons, color pens or pencils, or even highlighters, and color in how you are feeling. For example, let's say your wrist is in pain when you type. Color the wrist red and write the word "type" next to it. Write all the activities next to the painful area that make it hurt. Try to anticipate the doctor's questions. He will probably ask about radiating pain, so if your fingers also hurt, but only occasionally, color them orange. Again, write the activities that cause that discomfort next to the area.

Use the following colors or create your own color code:

Red: intense pain
Orange: minor pain
Yellow: discomfort or stiffness
Green: stuffiness
Blue: numbness
Black: heaviness

If you do this at home, take time in the waiting room to review your chart and add to it, if need be. Write specific questions on the bottom or the back of this paper and take it into the examining room. It will not only help you be more specific in your answers to the doctor, but it will also help the doctor with the diagnosis.

After treatment has begun, take time every day to color in an additional person and watch the amazing transformation from illness to health. This ritual can be done for long-term illnesses and their treatment as well. If that is the case, color in your image once a week or even once a month instead of every day. Once you have completed treatment and are completely well, burn the papers with the following admonition:

I am healthy in body and wealthy in health.

If you are not ill and are going to the doctor for a checkup, physical, or some other well-person exam, you can use the same ritual—modified. Take a copy of your outline, but leave it blank if you have no complaints. If the doctor tells you that something about your habits or general health needs to change—if you need more exercise, for example—then write that on your blank person. Pin it up at home to remind you that health is something actively sought, not passively accepted.

May good health be yours all the days of your life!

For Women Only

This section is for those situations that are unique to women's health. Women tend to find themselves in more "embarrassing" situations than men do during physical exams and yearly checkups. They also tend to see doctors more often. For all you women out there, this section is for you.

Getting a Pap Smear

A visit to the doctor is bad enough, but getting a Pap smear can be one of the most embarrassing situations women face while there. Even for the least modest among you, lying flat on your back with your legs in the air while a doctor examines your most private area puts you in an incredibly vulnerable position. Doctors know this and have tried a variety of things to help you feel more comfortable: decorated rooms with music playing, funny posters or sayings on the ceiling, even conversation that tries to take you away from what is happening. And all of this works . . . to some degree. Perhaps this ritual will add a little extra help.

Start this ritual the day you make your appointment and do it every day until you actually go to the doctor. This time frame can be as little as a day or as long as six weeks. It all depends on your doctor. It is the act of making the appointment that will be your reminder to begin. Lie on your back and put your legs in the examining position. Feel the position of your body. Now, stand up and try to emulate that position. You will find yourself in a squatting position with your feet far apart and pointing outward.

While in that position, try to think of a sport in which you would find yourself in a similar position—water skiing perhaps. The position you take in the water before the boat begins moving is very much like this squat. Rock climbing puts you in this position also, for it provides you with a great amount of stability if you are hanging off the side of a mountain. Vary this position slightly with your toes pointing in instead of out and you will find yourself a beginning snow skier, snow plowing to a stop. Like to ride a motorcycle? I bet you find yourself in this position when getting on or off your bike or while stopped at a light. Walking on the deck of a sailboat, you tend to stay low and move with your feet apart, for that position provides the greatest stability on a moving deck, even if it does make you look like a crab. The same is true for surfing and windsurfing, horseback riding too. Even a piece of equipment in horseback riding has the same name as the equipment in the doctor's office.

Whatever sport you pick, make it something you really enjoy doing or have always dreamed of learning. The next time you are in the *stirrups* for your annual Pap smear, close your eyes and imagine yourself participating in that sport you love—far away from the doctor's office.

Dream away!

Getting a Mammogram/Breast Self-Exam

Even though getting a mammogram or doing a breast self-exam is considered preventive medicine, the reason *why* you do this is always in the back of your mind. Some women put off mammograms because of a fear that the doctor will find something wrong. If something is indeed wrong, it is always better to know sooner rather than later. Your doctor or nurse can show you how to do a breast self-exam. There are also a number of websites that illustrate the proper technique. So there is no excuse *not* to perform this simple procedure. This ritual will help you overcome the discomfort of a mammogram and any reluctance you may feel about performing monthly self-exams by shifting your focus from yourself to an inanimate object.

You will need a large bag (one-pound size) of frozen creamed corn. Don't laugh, this really works. The day before your exam, take the corn from the freezer and put it in the refrigerator. Contrary to what you've been told, the mammogram machine is cold but it is not *ice* cold. Once the creamed corn is defrosted it should be slightly mushy and very similar to the way your breast feels. Place the cold bag over your naked breast. This will be about as cold as the mammogram machine. You should do this in a locked room; standing naked in the kitchen with a bag of creamed corn on your breast may cause consternation among family members.

Now do your self-exam. Compare the bag to your breast. They will feel similar. Switch. If you find something in your breast that would be like a rock in that bag of corn or something larger than a whole kernel of corn, you definitely should visit your doctor. Don't wait! I found something once that was a little larger than a pea and it turned out to be only a cyst, but I was relieved sooner rather than later by telling my doctor about it right away.

Before each mammogram or gynecologist appointment do this ritual. On the day of your appointment, wear your most comfortable shirt. If you can go braless, do so. Wear a loose camisole or chemise instead. This will help you feel less constricted. If you must wear a bra, make it your most comfortable one; leave the underwire push-up bra in your drawer at home. While your doctor, nurse, or technician is performing your exam, imagine that what they are examining is your refrigerated bag of creamed corn. If you end up laughing, you may want to share the joke with them. Who knows, they may share it with other patients. How wonderful that would be! Your ritual might help other women feel more comfortable while being examined.

After your exam, make some time to go shopping, perhaps with women friends. Buy yourself a pretty new blouse or a lacy bra to celebrate the fact that you made it through another exam.

Wear it in good health!

Menopause Onset

The symptoms of menopause begin long before menopause actually occurs. The hot flashes, mood swings, and physical changes signal that your childbearing days are coming to a close. The degree of upset at this eventuality varies greatly among women. Some see it as no great loss and are relieved to be done with it while others view it as a large part of their life ending and this latter group may grieve deeply. In many ancient cultures, the women who were past childbearing were considered the wise ones, or Crones, of the village and were sought out for their advice. It was generally accepted that these women were now holding on to their wisdom (their blood), instead of either passing it on to their children or passing it from their bodies. This ritual honors the wisdom of the Crone—the women who no longer bleed monthly. Start this ritual the first month after the cessation of your period.

Have a box of whatever sanitary item you use (pads or tampons), a writing pad and pen, and a fine point marker. Wrap a box with a removable lid, for you will be opening it periodically. Put a big bow and fancy ribbon on it along with a gift tag that says: "To: The Community at Large and Future Generations."

Find a quiet space to be alone for an hour or so and contemplate what you have to offer the world. Brainstorm and create a list of what you can give to others. Write down the elaborate ideas that come to mind as well as the simple ones. Make them ideas that can be passed on to or benefit others. Think grandmotherly. Here are some ideas to get you started in the right direction:

- Teach adults how to read.
- Read stories to schoolchildren.

- Create a cookbook of your favorite recipes for family members.

- Pass on your quilting secrets to a friend who has always wanted to learn.

- Teach a neighbor how to knit.

- Research your family tree.

- Put together photo albums for your kids.

- Write down stories of your favorite family member from a generation previous to yours.

- Teach someone how to be politically active.

- Become active in a grassroots campaign for a cause you believe in.

Any volunteer activity that passes on knowledge you have that others lack is appropriate. After you have come up with a *long* list, choose the top twelve items. Now, take twelve pads or tampons and write a key word on each one that will remind you of the wisdom you wish to pass on. Place the entire list in the bottom of the wrapped box and place the twelve pads or tampons on top of the list, then put the lid on the box.

Since natural menopause happens slowly, there will be months when you have periods and months when you don't. On the months that you don't have a period, open the box and give a gift of yourself. Choose, at random, one of the pads or tampons. Make an effort to spend the few days that you would normally bleed on that project. That time frame can be anywhere from three to seven days. What a way to spend your time. Sharing your special skills and abilities with others—from total strangers to close friends and family members.

After you have been through all the pads or tampons, you will find your original list at the bottom of the box. Review it. By this time you will have discovered what you prefer to pass on and what you don't. Find something new on the list and try it. Continue to pass on your knowledge. As the box empties, you will be satisfied that your skills and your knowledge will benefit the following generations for years to come.

Thank you for sharing your gift with others.

9

It's How You Play the Game

THERE ARE A FEW more rituals I wish to include that don't seem to fit into any of the previous chapters, but are nonetheless important. Some of these are the broader generalities of life, like dealing with stress; others are unique happenings like a specific lesson learned. These rituals are truly not about winning or losing but about playing the game. What is the game, you may ask? Why, life, of course!

New Course of Study

There are so many elements to learning something new that you may feel overwhelmed at first. As in cooking, you'll be bringing together all the ingredients needed to make a great meal. When you first learn to cook, you've got an appetizer, main course, and dessert to think about. As you get better, you may add soups, salads, and different wines for each course. Keep this in mind as you embark on your new course of study. Whether it is learning to paint or returning to school for that long-sought-after master's degree, this ritual should help.

Remember learning to drive? I bet you thought you would never remember all the different things required for that "simple" task. Let's run through them.

Get in car.
Adjust seat.
Check and adjust mirrors.
Fasten seat belt.
Put key in ignition.
Pump gas pedal a couple of times.
Turn key.
Start car.
Check emergency brake.
If emergency brake is set, release it.
Place foot on brake.
Check behind you and to the side.
Push in clutch.
Put car in reverse.
Move foot from brake to gas.
Slowly let out clutch and press gas.
Keep steering wheel straight as you back out.
Turn wheel and maneuver car out of parking space.
When the car is in the clear, depress clutch and move
      foot from gas to brake.
Stop car.
Shift to first gear.
Move foot from brake to gas.

Slowly let out clutch and press gas.
Turn wheel to straighten out car.

Congratulations! You're out of your parking place. Actually driving on the road is even more complicated. Or is it? It was when you first learned to drive. You consciously thought about the above list. With experience and sheer repetition, driving became easier. Somewhere along the way, it got to the point that you no longer thought about the individual components, you just got in the car and drove wherever you needed to go.

During your new learning experience, read through the above list when you feel bogged down in the details of whatever you are learning. This will help you realize that whatever you are studying is not as complicated as it may seem. And just like the day you looked back and realized you could drive without thinking too much about it, you will find yourself at that same point in your new studies.

Remember, learning something new should be fun and exciting. Otherwise, why do it? Have fun, and you will soon be proficient in your new skill.

Lesson Learned

Whenever we learn a particularly difficult lesson, we tend to look back and say, "*Duh!*" Seriously, though, hindsight is ever perfect. It doesn't matter which lesson you learned, although here I am talking about a lesson that has broader implications in your life than a school course, the kind of lesson that has a broad impact on your life. That lesson could have been about correcting certain work habits that had been holding you back in your career. Or you could have finally realized that you could be healthy without going to the gym every day—three times a week was enough. Any moment in your life when you have been hit by the spiritual two-by-four without getting knocked out is a moment to celebrate. So no matter what the lesson was that you learned, do this short ritual in celebration.

Sit in your car for a few moments and look at your reflection in the rearview mirror. If you don't have a car, this ritual can be done at home with a small hand-held mirror. Position yourself in front of a window where you can see outside. Think about the lesson you just learned and how those mistakes you made in the past led you to where you are now— beyond that particular trouble. By seeing your reflection in conjunction with what is behind you, you can see how things have developed and come to the realization that the things most worth learning are the things that are the most difficult to attain. The hard part is over and now it's time to move on and leave the past behind.

Shift your focus to the windshield or window and, once again, focus on your image in that glass. It's not as clear, is it? That's because the future isn't set like the past. Put your hands on the wheel or the window and imagine where you can go in your life now that you wouldn't have been able to without learning the lesson you just did. Now, look beyond your reflection, literally and figuratively. By doing this you are shifting your focus from the past to the future. Visualize where you want to go and how you want to get there. Know that knowledge gained and the lesson learned is like the car in which you sit. With gas (your will), maintenance (your health), and a roadmap (your imagination) you can go any-where you want.

Congratulations on surviving the cosmic two-by-four. Now, hit the gas!

Speaking in Public

There are few people who *don't* get nervous at the thought of speaking in public. Even experienced, professional perform-ers sometimes find their voices quavering and their palms sweaty. It is said that Frank Sinatra used to get physically ill before each performance. So don't feel bad if you, an ordi-nary person, get totally freaked out at the thought of speak-ing in public. If you can get past those first few moments, everything typically settles down and you "get into" the topic at hand. This ritual is designed to distract you just enough to get you past that first wave of fear as you step onto that stage or take your position in front of a roomful of board members.

There's an old joke that goes something like this. A musician has a gig, but he can't find the hall where he is performing, so he asks a passer-by: "Excuse me, how do you get to Carnegie Hall?" The fellow answers, "Practice, practice, prac-tice." This well-used bit of advice is also the beginning of your ritual for speaking in public—practice. Practice often and in front of a lot of different people. It is easier to talk to five hundred strangers than it is to five of your closest friends. If you can get over your nervousness giving your speech or making your presentation to a family member, then talking to an audience will be a piece of cake.

Take your rehearsal one step further and practice in front of a mirror. Watch your facial expressions and make eye contact as much as possible: this shows you are unafraid and sincere.

The night before your big presentation, rehearse in front of the mirror one last time and get your notes in the right order. Pick out the clothes you will wear the next day. Choose an outfit that is as comfortable as it is appropriate to the occasion. Tugging at a tie that is too tight or fidgeting with a blouse that won't stay tucked in will distract you, as well as your audience, from your presentation. Wear shoes that are comfortable as well, you will most likely be standing most of the time and shifting your weight from foot to foot causes your audience to wonder just how sure you are in what you are presenting.

On the big day, try to distract yourself from constantly reviewing your speech. Choose an activity that is completely different from what you will be speaking on. Don't worry. You have practiced and rehearsed. You have notes and materials to help you and to remind you of your direction. If you focus too much on your speech right before giving it, you may end up second guessing yourself and changing things at the last minute that don't need to be changed.

Just before you walk out on stage or into the conference room, take several deep breaths and let them out with an audible sigh. This releases tension from your body and from your voice. It also calms your racing heart. Just remember, fear and excitement are the same chemical reaction in your body. It is your attitude that determines which emotion is experienced.

When you begin your speech, "see" your mirror in front of you. As you meet the eyes of the people sitting in the room, see your own eyes staring back at you, or the eyes of your loved ones. If you are talking to a large audience, look around the auditorium occasionally. Even though you cannot truly make eye contact with people so far away, it will appear that you can and that you are speaking to the entire assemblage and not just those in the middle or in the first couple of rows.

Anytime the fear returns, "imagine" that mirror in front of you and that you are in your home, practicing.

Good luck! You'll do great!

Dealing with Stress

Stress. It creeps into all our lives from time to time—problems at work, falling grades, relationship problems. All the negatives in our lives tend to build on themselves and become overwhelming. But stress is also caused by the good things that happen in our lives, such as weddings, a new home, or a great opportunity in a new city. Whatever the causes of your stress, this ritual is designed not to make them go away, but to help you put them into perspective and, maybe, even make them smaller and a little fun.

We all have personal ways of overcoming stress—a long chat with a friend, watching a favorite movie, taking a long walk, soaking in a hot tub. Whatever way you deal with stress, please continue, but add this short ritual to what you already do.

When problems go round and round in our heads, they tend to appear larger than they truly are. It's kind of like a snowball rolling downhill, getting larger as it goes. This ritual throws it in the air instead.

When you *speak* a problem, it takes power away from it. So get yourself a bottle of bubbles from your local toy store. Take it outside and blow a bubble for each thing in your life that is causing you stress. Speak that stress into the bubble. Watch it float for a while. Gee, it isn't as heavy as you thought, is it? When the bubble pops, imagine the stress disappearing with it. That doesn't mean that the *problem* has gone away, only that the stress associated with it has. Stress has a wonderful way of freezing us up and making it difficult to move. We have trouble even beginning to tackle the problem that has caused it.

When you finally tackle that problem, picture the bubble in your mind and watch it pop! It just may free you from inertia and uncertainty. One of my favorite quotes is taped to my computer. It is by Dorthea Brande and it reads: "All that is necessary to break the spell of inertia is this: Act as if it were impossible to fail." Seeing that bubble float helps break the spell of inertia. Seeing it pop releases you from its influence and your frustration. And it will probably make you smile.

So anytime stress builds up on the inside, take it outside, release it from your body, and play with it.

May all your stresses float away with ease!

Dealing with Anger

Anger. The offspring of frustration and injustice. It is one of the more insidious emotions and a dangerous one as well. It comes on you out of nowhere and sometimes refuses to leave. The "fight or flight" response kicks in and makes your heart race, your palms sweat, your vision blur. It also has a tendency to impair your judgment and can cause you to say or do things you would never ordinarily do. If you are a parent, you know the value of the "time-out" corner—a place you send your child to cool off after an argument or to think about his disobedience. As adults we have lost not only the physicality of the time-out corner, but the concept of it as well. The following ritual brings back that idea and gives you a constructive and safe outlet for your anger, but on a much smaller scale.

One positive thing that anger does is it gives us a lot of energy, that fight-or-flight response again. If we can find an outlet for that energy, we can not only release it, but use it to our advantage.

Have a craft corner in your home that you can retreat to when you are feeling angry. Make that craft something that requires a lot of physical effort, but very little thought. Do you like to create mosaics? Save the big tiles for a time when you are angry, then get the hammer, use that anger, and break those tiles into tiny bits. Sand that unfinished table with furious strokes. Wash the car. Paint the house. Think I'm joking? I painted an entire room in my house in an *after-noon* on a day when I was really angry. Of course I got more paint on myself than on the wall at times, but my anger dissipated and I could think clearly again by the end of the day. Not only that, I had a freshly painted room to enjoy.

You can do this at the office as well, but it obviously needs to be on a much smaller scale. Do you have papers that need to be shredded? Shred them with your hands during a moment of anger. The ripping and tearing sounds can be very satisfying. One of those little rubber balls you can manipulate is helpful also. (Someone was really thinking when they designed those.) If you can leave your desk, take a short, brisk walk outside. Pick up rocks and throw them with all your might across an empty field. Kick a can all the way back to the office and then throw it away. Not only have you released some of your anger, there is one less piece of trash outside.

Allow yourself to be angry and your anger will dissipate much faster. Be creative with it and use it to your advantage and you will find yourself "blowing off steam" without offending anyone. Good luck!

Searching for Inspiration

We all have days when we feel the need for some inspiration and for whatever reason, we cannot find it from our regular sources. Maybe a special project is stagnating. Maybe your relationship needs an extra something. Whatever you need inspiration for, look to this list of small rituals to help you out of your funk.

All these rituals are nature based for the simple reason that the most awe-inspiring details can be found in the great outdoors. If you are searching for inspiration during certain seasons, look to the weather outside. Actually, during any time of year, you can look to weather for inspiration or simply look to the sky.

Spring. It is easiest to be inspired in the Spring when you see what was apparently dead come back to life. The brilliance of the blossoms echoes the brilliance of your own ideas.

Summer. Go outside just before sunset and explore the colors in the sky as night approaches. Imagine how each of those colors could relate to the situation at hand. As dusk falls, watch the fireflies signal to one another. Visualize that each brilliant flash is an idea expressly for you. Ask the firefly what it is trying to tell you.

Autumn. Take a walk among the falling leaves and imagine that each leaf that touches you is inspiration being given you by the trees themselves. Pick up leaves along the way and examine the intricacies of the pattern of veins and colors.

Winter. See the bare branches of the trees as the bare bones of your ideas and know that the structure must be there before the leaves and blossoms fill in the details. While it is snowing, remember what you learned as a child that each snowflake is unique. Know that each idea you have is also unique.

Sunny, cloudless days. See the open sky as your open mind and encourage the rays of the sun to take their place in your thoughts.

Clouds. See the clouds as ideas floating by. Relive childhood memories by seeking shapes within the clouds. This will help you see the shapes in your own mind as those ideas transfer from the sky to your mind.

Stars. Let each bright distant light be a solution or an idea that has come from across the cosmos to take shape in your plans.

The moon. Each generation falls in love with the moon and her endlessly changing face. She encourages change in you, too, illuminating your darkest hours with her soft, subtle light.

Rain. Each drop of rain could be an idea for your project. Watch the rain and see how it reacts with different surfaces; it splatters on a window, it splashes in a puddle, it gently falls on the soft earth and immediately soaks in. Visualize yourself as the earth and the rain as your inspiration.

Thunderstorms. These are the ideas that strike out of nowhere and illuminate your mind with thoughts so intense they could knock you out of your chair.

Blizzards, tornadoes, hurricanes, windstorms. These whirlwinds of ideas block out all distractions and carry you away to a place where you can get totally lost in your thoughts.

Fog. Fog focuses your senses on the ideas in your mind that are not the most obvious, just as fog forces you to use smell or hearing instead of sight. Focus on the foghorn as the source of your inspiration and let it lead you to your idea.

Use nature as your inspiration and you will never run out of ideas. Every blade of grass is unique. Each peach on a tree has a slightly different taste. Revel in your difference instead of seeing yourself as the same, and inspiration will surely be yours.

Dream on!

Gratitude

How many times have you said to yourself, "I sure am glad
_____ happened" or "I am relieved _____ didn't happen."
Gratitude is not just about what you receive, but also what
you *don't* receive. The morning after a party, you may rise to
a house that looks as though a tornado crashed through it.
But as you clean, you find yourself with fond remembrances
of the evening and you are grateful for such good friends.
Finding out that a lump in your breast is *not* cancer creates
not only a sense of relief, but one of gratitude as well. Try
this ritual of thanksgiving when you find yourself grateful
for the things that are both in your life and *not* in your life.

This ritual is an ongoing one that not only celebrates the
things you are grateful for, but can also help you through the
times when you feel you have nothing and that life is being
particularly unfair, or that things you love are being taken
away.

The first thing you will need is a basket, preferably one in
the shape of a cornucopia. Your local craft store or home
decorating shop should have one, and if by chance it is close
to Thanksgiving when you begin this ritual, you should
be able to find one without a great deal of effort. If you
cannot find one in the shape of a cornucopia then draw that
image on a sheet of paper and attach it to the side of the
basket you are using. This is your basket of gratitude. Keep it
in an honored place in your home, a place where you will
see it often. It is meant to remind you not only to be grateful,
but also to help you realize all that you are grateful *for*.

Every time you find yourself grateful for something in

your life, write it down on a piece of paper along with the date and put it in this basket. Start out with the major things in life you are grateful for: good health, a loving spouse, a job you enjoy, a comfortable home, faithful friends.

Don't limit yourself to the large things in life, though. Be grateful for the little things also: a favorite sweater, a fascinating book, a tasty meal, a night at the movies, a beautiful Spring day.

Focus on the positive aspects of negative happenings as well. For example: If you have to take your car in to be repaired, be thankful that it doesn't have to be replaced. You could also be grateful for someone who offers you a ride while your car is in the shop. Be thankful that the shop washed or vacuumed your car after it was worked on. Most of all, be grateful that you now have a working vehicle. It's quite a challenge to get into this habit, but once you do, you will start to see life in a much more positive way.

On days when you feel life is particularly unfair, pull a handful of papers from your cornucopia and read them. Not only will it brighten your day, it will help you focus on the good in your life. Once a year take all of the papers out of your cornucopia and read them all. You could do this on the traditional day of gratitude—Thanksgiving. This ritual could also be performed on your birthday, or the first day of the year—appropriate times to read about all the good in your life.

After you have finished reading all you have been thankful for through the year, bundle the papers with a rubber band or paperclip and put them back into your cornucopia. Start adding to them again with a paper that says you are grateful for all that the past year has given you. Continue this ritual and don't worry about duplication. Every time you are thankful for a loving spouse or sympathetic friend, put it in the basket. In another year read them again. By doing this continual ritual, you will find yourself becoming even more grateful for the wonderful things in your life and your cornucopia will overflow.

Happy Thanksgiving! Every day!

EPILOGUE

The Final Ritual

NOW THAT WE'VE REACHED the end of *Life's Little Rituals* you can see that a ritual can take many different forms. It is the intent with which you perform these everyday celebrations that makes them into rituals. The importance of ritual is overlooked in our day-to-day lives; that is why I wrote this book.

One more ritual will make this book complete. It is a ritual of your own making. Following is the template I used in creating these rituals for you. I wish to share it with you so you can create your own rituals for any occasion that may arise in your life.

First ask yourself a few questions and write down your answers.

What makes this occasion special *to me*?
How can I add meaning to this event?
What is the purpose of this happening?

Next, shift your focus from the practical to the ceremonial and the symbolic. The best way to do this is by thinking of analogies for your special occasion. You can use the elements, animals, colors, children's games. Anything that can represent the main focus of your ritual. Think similes. You are brainstorming here, so write down *all* your ideas. There will be one or two that will stand out when you are finished.

Take that representation and add words and action. Think of the physical, mental, and emotional reactions to the purpose of your ritual.

End your ritual with a statement of the conscious intent.

There. Now that wasn't terribly difficult, was it?

By ritualizing everyday life, we end up with "the meaning of life" . . . A life filled with meaning.